365
Prayers
for the Family

Magpie Books, London

Constable & Robinson Ltd
3 The Lanchesters
162 Fulham Palace Road
London W6 9ER
www.constablerobinson.com

This edition published by Magpie Books,
an imprint of Constable & Robinson Ltd 2005

ISBN 1 84529 193 X

Compiled by Diane Law

A copy of the British Library Cataloguing in
Publications Data is available from the British Library

Printed and bound in the EU

365
Prayers
for the Family

Christian

A blessing before meals

Bless us,
O Lord,
And these thy gifts,
Which we are about to receive from thy
    bounty,
Through Christ, our Lord,
Amen.

Gaelic

Deep peace

Deep peace of the running wave to you,
Deep peace of the quiet earth to you,
Deep peace of the flowing air to you,
Deep peace of the shining star to you.

Christian

A prayer for mothers

To mothers You have given
    the great privilege and responsibility
    of being a child's first teacher and spiritual
    guide.
Help mothers to grow daily in knowledge and
    understanding of Your Son, Our Lord Jesus
    Christ.
We ask your blessing on all those to whom
    You have entrusted motherhood.
May Your Holy Spirit constantly inspire and
    strengthen them.
May they ever follow the example of Mary,
    mother of Our Lord, and imitate her self-
    giving love.
We ask this through our Lord and Savior,
    Jesus Christ.
Amen.

Christian

Grace after meals

We give thee thanks, almighty God, for all
   your benefits, who livest and reignest
   forever and ever.
May the Lord grant us His peace.
And life everlasting.
Amen.

Christian

Glory be to the father

Glory be to the Father
And to the Son and to the Holy Spirit.
As it was in the beginning,
Is now and ever shall be,
World without end.
Amen.

Christian

Morning prayers

O my God,
I offer unto Thee all my thoughts, works, joys,
   and sufferings of this day.
And I beseech Thee to grant me Thy grace
   that I may not offend Thee this day; but
   may faithfully serve Thee and do Thy holy
   will in all things.
Amen.

Christian

Blessing

May the Lord bless us,
And keep us from evil,
And bring us unto everlasting life.
Amen.

Jewish

A prayer for the world

Let the rain come and wash away the ancient
grudges, the bitter hatreds held and
nurtured over generations.
Let the rain wash away the memory of the
hurt, the neglect.
Then let the sun come out and fill the sky
with rainbows.
Let the warmth of the sun heal us wherever we
are broken.
Let it burn away the fog so that we can see
each other clearly.
Let the warmth and brightness of the sun melt
our selfishness.
And let the light of the sun be so strong that
we will see all people as our neighbors.
Let the earth, nourished by rain, bring forth
flowers to surround us with beauty.
And let the mountains teach our hearts to
reach upward to heaven.
Amen.

Rabbi Harold S. Kushner

Christian

A prayer for fathers

Most gracious Heavenly Father,
We thank you for our earthly fathers, those to
    whom you have entrusted the responsibility
    to provide loving protection of their
    families and guidance of their children.
May our earthly fathers imitate the manly
    courage of Abraham, Jesse and Joseph, in
    providing wise counsel to the children you
    have given to their care.
We ask your blessing on all those to whom
    you have entrusted fatherhood.
May your Holy Spirit constantly inspire them
    with justice and mercy, wisdom and
    strength, fidelity and self-giving love.
May they receive your grace abundantly in this
    earthly life, and look forward to eternal joy
    in your presence in the life to come.
Through Jesus Christ, your Son and Our Lord.
Amen.

Jewish

A grateful heart

Though I walk amid distress,
You preserve me; against the anger of my
    enemies.
You raise Your hand; Your right hand saves
    me.
The Lord will complete what He has done for
    me.
Your kindness, O Lord, endures forever.
Forsake not the work of Your hands.

Psalm 137

Christian

A seasonal prayer

The chill in the air and the turning of the
    leaves brings us a new season.
God, we ask you to renew our spirit.
Let our family actions speak the truth of your
    love.
Let those who see us know you a little better.
This we ask through your Son and the Holy
    Spirit.
Amen.

Buddhist

Loving kindness prayer

May I be free from fear; may I be free from
    suffering.
May I be happy; may I be filled with loving
    kindness.

Christian

A family thanksgiving prayer

Thank you, God, for the gift of our family.
Be with us in our good times and in our
   struggles.
Help us be always conscious of the love we
   have for each other.
Let us reflect on the many blessings You have
   given us.
In the name of Jesus Christ Our Lord.
Amen.

Hindu

Morning prayer

May all in this world be happy.
May they all be healthy, be comfortable and
   never miserable.
May the rain come down in the proper time.
May the earth yield plenty of corn, and may
   the country be free from war.

Christian

For our children and grandchildren

Lord, thank You for sending us each child.
Thank You for protecting them all today.
Turn their hearts and minds towards You and
   towards pleasing you.
For Jesus Christ Your Holy Son.
Amen.

Christian

Prayer for protection

The light of God surrounds me;
The love of God enfolds me;
The power of God protects me;
The presence of God watches over me;
Wherever I am, God is.

Islamic

Bedtime prayer

In Thy name, Lord, I lay me down and in
 Thy name will I rise up.
O God, Thou art the first and before Thee
 there is nothing;
Thou art the last and after Thee there is
 nothing;
Thou art the outmost and above Thee there is
 nothing;
Thou art the inmost and below Thee there is
 nothing.
Waken me, O God, in the hour most pleasing
 to Thee and use me in the works most
 pleasing to Thee.

Shamanistic

For the gift of children

Thank you, Our Creator, for the Sacred Gift
   of Children.

Help us all to honor this Sacred Gift of Family
   in our thoughts and in our behavior.

Help us to see them in the Light of Love and
   Forgiveness and Appreciation.

Help us to treat them with respect and with
   kindness.

Thank you for their touch in our lives, the
   gifts of their teachings, and at times their
   testing.

Bless them, wherever they may be, in body or
   in Spirit, with the awareness that they are
   loved.

Bless them with your protection.

And finally, help us all to grow in our
   awareness so that we are all joined together
   in your Heart of Infinite Love.

With your help, may it be so.

Christian

A daily prayer

Lord, help me live from day to day
In such an humble sort of way,
To give a smile, help lift a load
For those I meet along life's road.
And when I come to my journey's end,
My life I have not lived in vain,
If one dear friend can smile and say
I'm glad I met her on life's way.

Christian

Prayer of thanksgiving

For health and strength and daily food,
We praise your name, O God.
Amen.

Shamanistic

For the winter solstice

To our Great Spirit, Our Creator, who has
   been forever and will be forever.
We open our hearts and send our voice to you
   with thankfulness for the gifts of winter.
Our Mother Earth takes the bodies of the
   fallen leaves from autumn and in her depth
   converts their energy into food for the life
   that will come forth in the births of
   springtime.
Help us to listen to the dreaming you send
   into us during these long winter months.
For with your help and guidance, may we use
   it well.
With your help, may it be so.

Islamic

For obedience

Lord, you do not put a greater burden on a
   soul than it can bear.
You are not angry with us when we make
   mistakes, but are quick to forgive us and set
   us right.
You do not lead us into moral and spiritual
   danger without protecting and guiding us,
   so our souls can emerge unscathed.
You do not allow us to be defeated by the
   deceits of unbelievers, but ensure that
   ultimately truth will be victorious.
Lord, we listen to you, and we obey you.

Prophet Mohammed, 570–632,
Founder of Islam

Christian

Blessing at mealtimes

Thank you for the food we eat,
Thank you for the friends we meet.
Thank you for the birds that sing,
Thank you, God, for everything.
Amen.

Hindu

Tears of love

O my Lord, when will my eyes be decorated
with tears of love flowing constantly
when I chant Your holy name?
When will my voice choke up, and
when will the hairs of my body stand on end
at the recitation of Your name?

Christian

Joy at a new birth

To our loving God,
Morning has come again into our lives.
The sunshine of a new birth brightens our
   entire family.
We pray for your help, to guide this child's life
   in your ways.
Help us so this child will flourish, be always
   aware of our love
And always aware of your love.
Amen.

Shamanistic

For peace and health

To the Power of the West,
Thank you for the gifts of inner peace, light
    and love, courage and compassion, healing
    and forgiveness.
Give me the strength to overcome my
    weakness and to honor the powers I have
    been given in this life.
Let them be brought out successfully in the
    world for healing.
With your help, may it be so.

Islamic

Prayer for parents

My Lord! Please bestow on them thy Mercy
    even as they cherished me in childhood.

Surah 17: Al-Isra (The Night Journey): 24

Jewish

Morning meditation

I give thanks to You, living and everlasting
   King, for you have returned my soul to me
   with compassion.
Great is your faithfulness.
Amen.

American Indian

For she who heals

Mother, sing me a song
That will ease my pain,
Mend broken bones,
Bring wholeness again.
Catch my babies
When they are born,
Sing my death song,
Teach me how to mourn.
Show me the medicine
Of the healing herbs,
The value of spirit,
The way I can serve.
Mother, heal my heart
So that I can see
The gifts of yours
That can live through me.

Christian

At a time of illness

Lord, I pray to return to good health and ask
    for the strength to bear this burden.
Help me to remember your sacrifice on the
    cross and that all things pass in time, and
    serve to bring us closer to you.
Amen.

Christian

Blessing of the Christmas tree

Our Lord God,
You brought your son, Jesus, to teach us the
    power of love and sacrifice.
As we raise this tree, let us remember his birth
    and the meaning of his life.
Bless our tree as a symbol of celebration of
    Jesus' birth and our gratitude for his
    sacrifice.
May the joy this tree brings and the gifts we
    place under it remind us of the many gifts
    you have given to us.
Please place your blessings upon our loved
    ones, on this day and always.
That we may follow your path,
Amen.

Shamanistic

Prayer for all which is feminine

To our mother the Great Goddess.
Thank you for your light and your
    unconditional love.
Thank you for the gift of the feminine energy,
    the gift of feeling and of intuition.
Thank you for your strength, always pouring
    out your love no matter what.
Thank you for always being there.
Help me to open myself to your compassion
    and tenderness.
Help me to bring it in to the places within me
    and to be a channel for your healing,
With your help, may it be so.

Christian

Mealtime blessing

Lord, as we gather we give you thanks for the
food that the earth has provided.
We praise the hands that have made it and
take delight in the gifts you have given.
We ask you to bless this bountiful food to our
bodies.
We ask this in your name Jesus Christ.
Amen.

Christian

Morning prayer

Lord Jesus Christ, we praise you and thank
  you for this new day.
As morning dawns, we ask you to hear our
  prayer.
No matter where we go and what we do, we
  ask your unfailing protection.
Watch over our children with your tender care
  as they journey to school today.
Guide us all in faith so that we might share
  the gospel with all those we meet.
Make us strong so that we may bear witness to
  the gospel in all that we do.
We ask this in your name Our Lord Jesus.
Amen.

Christian

Evening prayer

Let us pray.
From the beginning of the day until its end,
    we are grateful for your love.
We thank you for watching over us today.
We praise you for the courage to be merciful
    with our family, friends and co-workers and
    ask you to show mercy toward us.
Through your love make us whole and bring
    us to new life.
We make this prayer through Christ Jesus.
Amen.

Christian (traditional)

Mealtime grace

Before we eat this food, dear Lord,
We bow our heads to pray;
And for your blessings and your care
Our humble thanks we say.
Amen.

North American Indian

Mealtime thanksgiving

Now that I am about to eat,
O Great Spirit, give my thanks to the beasts
    and birds whom You have provided for my
    hunger;
And pray deliver my sorrow that living things
    must make a sacrifice for my comfort and
    well-being.
Let the feather of corn spring up in its time
    and let it not wither but make full grains
    for the fires of our cooking pots, now that I
    am about to eat.

Islamic

To have a healthy child

O my Lord! Grant unto me from Thee a
    progeny that is pure
For Thou art He that hears my prayer.

Surah 3: Aal-E-Imran
(The Family of Imran): 38

Christian

A death in the family

Dear Lord,
Help us to understand this pain that comes
into our lives when we lose someone we
love.
Help us to remember that life is a circle.
You have given us eternal life.
In dying, our loved one is returned to you as
will we all in time.
Help us to see that this sadness brings us to
our greatest happiness.
Bless, with your presence, those we love and
miss.
Amen.

Christian

In seeking God during difficult times

O God, you are my God.
Early will I seek you.
My flesh longs for you,
My soul thirsts for you,
In a barren and dry land where there is no water.

Psalm 63: 1

Islamic

For obedient worship

O my Lord! make me one who establishes
   regular Prayer, and also raise such among
   my offspring.
Accept Thou my Prayer.
Cover us with Thy Forgiveness, me, my
   parents, and all.

Surah 14: Ibrahim (Abraham): 40–41

Sikh

Prayer for peace

"God judges us according to our deeds, not
    the coat that we wear."
That Truth is above everything, but higher
    still is truthful living.
Know that we attain God when we love, and
    only that victory endures in consequence of
    which no one is defeated.

Shamanistic

For wisdom

To the Power of the North, Power of
Wisdom,
Thank you, Wisdom, for elders of all faiths
and traditions throughout time.
You who know that the Great Spirit's presence
is working for the greatest good in everyone,
everything, everywhere and all the time.
Thank you for your wisdom and guidance
whenever I turn to you with an open and
humble heart.
Help me to see the Spirit working for good in
all the challenges of my life.
With your help, may it be so.

Islamic

For guests

O my Lord! Forgive me, my parents,
Forgive all who enter my house in Faith, and
    all believing men and believing women;
To the wrong-doers grant Thou no increase
    but in perdition!

Surah 71: Nooh (Nooh): 28

Christian

Blessing for food

Lord Jesus Christ, be Thou our guest, and
    share the food which Thou hast blessed.
Amen.

Islamic

For fertility

O my Lord! leave me not without offspring,
Though thou art the best of inheritors.

Surah 21: Al-Anbiya (The Prophets): 89

Shamanistic

For family prosperity

Thank you for the gift of life, for being alive
here on our beautiful Mother Earth.

Thank you for the opportunity we have to
open up to you and to explore what true
prosperity really is – that which is found in
the heart.

Yours is a universe of plenty, but it is not for
the greedy or those with closed heart.

Love is for giving.

Help us to be love-finders and love-givers, to
ourselves, to others, to those less fortunate,
to life itself, to Mother Earth and to our
Great Creator.

Help us to find ways to meet our needs that
promote the vitality, diversity and
sustainability of life for all people.

Help us to cross the bridge of patience to the
prosperity of inner peace.

With your help, may it be so.

Christian

If afraid

To you alone, O Jesus, I must cling.
Running to your arms, dear Lord,
There let me hide, safe from all fears,
Loving you with the tenderness of a child.

After St Therese of Lisieux, 1873–97

Islamic

For family and marriage

Our Lord! Grant unto us wives and offspring
who will be the comfort of our eyes,
And give us the grace to lead the righteous.

Surah 25: Al-Furqan (The Criterion): 74

Christian

At a time of family conflict

Bless us Lord within this family when the
stresses of our lives cause us to bring each
other hurt and pain.
This is not the way we choose to live with
each other.
Still, all too often, it is how we are living.
Please guide us back to a better and more
loving way.
Help us to bury anger and return to the seed
of our love.
Help us to value each other as you value us.
May your presence give us the strength to heal
our rifts and help us to move forward.
Amen.

Jewish

Bedtime prayer

Blessed are you, Lord our God, king of the
universe, who causes the bonds of sleep to
fall on my eyes, and slumber on my eyelids.
May it be acceptable in your presence, O Lord
my God, to cause me to lie down in peace,
and to raise me up again in peace; and suffer
me not to be troubled with evil dreams, or
evil reflections.
Grant me a calm and uninterrupted repose in
your presence; and enlighten my eyes again,
lest I sleep the sleep of death.
Blessed are you, O Lord, who gives light to
the whole universe in your glory.
Amen.

Buddhist

A blessing

May every creature abound in well-being and
   peace.
May every living being, weak or strong, the
   long and the small,
The short and the medium-sized, the mean
   and the great,
May every living being, seen or unseen, those
   dwelling far off,
Those nearby, those already born, those
   waiting to be born,
May all attain inward peace.
Let no one deceive another.
Let no one despise another in any situation.
Let no one, from antipathy or hatred, wish
   evil to anyone at all.
Just as a mother, with her own life, protects
   her only son from hurt
So within yourself foster a limitless concern for
   every living creature.
Display a heart of boundless love for all the
   world.

In all its height and depth and broad extent
Love unrestrained, without hate or enmity.
Then as you stand or walk, sit or lie, until
    overcome by drowsiness
Devote your mind entirely to this, it is known
    as living here life divine.

The Buddha

Sikh

Sacred song

May the passions of lust, anger, greed, pride
    and attachment depart from me.
O Lord, I come to seek Thy shelter.
Bless me with Thy grace.

Shamanistic

Being thankful and asking for guidance

To our Creator, Source of All.
You have been always and you will be always.
You gave birth to me and will receive me
    when my life path is over as you have done
    for all the ancestors who have come before.
You are here now in my center and the center
    of all.
Thank you for this day and the opportunity to
    know you and to serve you.
Thank you for my family, friends, teachers,
    and loved ones.
Thank you for the work you give me to do in
    this life.
I pray for strength, Great Spirit, please help
    me to do the best I can do, to honor what I
    have seen to be true.
With your help, may it be so.

Islamic

Prayer for courage

Lord, put courage into my heart and take
   away all that may hinder me serving You.
Free my tongue to proclaim Your goodness,
   that all may understand me.
Give me friends to advise and help me, so that
   by working together our efforts may bear
   abundant fruit.
And, above all, let me constantly remember
   that all my actions are guided by Your
   hand.

Prophet Mohammed, 570–632,
Founder of Islam

Christian

In need of guidance

O Jesus, I have promised
To serve thee to the end,
Be thou for ever near me
My Master and my Friend
I shall not fear the battle
If thou art by my side,
Nor wander from the pathway
If thou wilt be my guide.

John E. Bode, 1816–64

Christian

For education

Good Jesus, you have deigned to refresh our
    souls with the sweet stream of knowledge;
    grant that one day we may come to you, its
    source and spring.

Alcuin of York, 735–804

Shamanistic

Prayer to give thanks

To our Creator of All.
Thank you for the sacred gift of the Life
Force.
Thank you for the gifts of your creation.
Thank you for this day and the opportunity to
know you and serve you.
Thank you for your presence always.
Thank you for your unconditional love and
forgiveness.
I place my future in your hands and choose to
experience inner peace now.
With your help, may it be so.

Islamic

Prayer for achievement

Lord, may everything that I do start well and
finish well.
Sustain me with your power.
And in your power let me drive away all
falsehood, ensuring that truth may always
triumph.

Prophet Mohammed, 570–632,
Founder of Islam

Christian

Lord, you have given me so much;
I ask for one more thing – a grateful heart.

George Herbert, 1593–1633

Christian

A Mother's Day prayer

Mary, mother of Jesus,
You formed your child's faith and led him to
   his destiny.
You lived your life in this world and became a
   model for all women.
On this special day, as in all the days of my
   life, I ask blessings for my mother and for
   all women in my life whose faith and care
   have blessed me.
Amen.

Sikh

Prayer for unity: prayer of the One

Some remember God as Ram;
   some call him Khuda;
Some use the name Gosain;
   some worship him as Allah.
Gracious Lord Almighty,
   you are the source and cause of everything,
O Lord, Compassionate One,
   shower your grace on all.
Some bathe at Hindu holy places;
   some go to perform the Hajj;
Some engage in Puja;
   some bow their heads in prayer;
Some study Vedas;
   some read the Bible or Qur'an.
Some dress in blue; some wear white;
Some call themselves Muslims;
   some are called Hindus.
Some desire to go to heaven;
   some long for paradise.
But whoever does the will of God,
To him all things are revealed.

Guru Nanak, 1469–1538,
Founder of the Sikh religion

Buddhist

A prayer for peace

May all beings everywhere, plagued with
  sufferings of body and mind soon be freed
  from their illnesses.
May those frightened cease to be afraid, and
  may those bound be free.
May the powerless find power, and may
  people think of befriending one another.
May those who find themselves in trackless,
  fearful wildernesses – the children, the aged,
  the unprotected – be guarded by beneficent
  celestials.

Christian

Praise and thanksgiving for help in times of trouble

Give thanks to the Lord, for he is good;
His loving kindness endures for ever,
I was hard pressed, and almost fell,
But the Lord helped me.
You are my God, and I will praise you.
You are my God, I will extol you.

Psalm 118: 1, 13, 28

Christian

In times of difficulty

Lord,
I am tearing the heart of my soul in two.
I need you to come
And lie there yourself
In the wounds of my soul.

Mechtild of Magdeburg, 1207–94

Shamanistic

For daylight

Father Sun, Power of the East,
Power of illumination.
Thank you for shining today, for giving away
    your light and your love, bringing the life
    force to Mother Earth.
Thank you for your power to cut through
    darkness.
Help us to cut through it and remember your
    light and love and to extend this to our
    families and all who cross our path today.
With your help, may it be so.

Hindu

Thanksgiving prayer for meals

This ritual is one.
The food is one.
We who offer the food are one.
The fire of hunger is also one.
All action is one.
We who understand this are one.

Christian

In times of difficulty

O Lord, hear my voice when I cry unto you;
Have mercy on me and answer me.
Do not hide your face from me;
Nor thrust me aside in displeasure:
For you are my helper; cast me not away;
Do not forsake me, O God of my salvation.

Psalm 27: 7,9

Hindu

A prayer for safety

Where the mind is without fear and the head
    is held high.
Where knowledge is free, where the world is
    not broken into fragments by wars.
Where words come from the depths of truth,
    where tireless striving stretches towards
    perfection.
Where the clear stream of reason has not lost
    its way into the dreary desert sand of habit;
Where the mind is led forward by thee into
    ever-widening thought and action;
Into that heaven of freedom, my Father, let
    my country awake.

Rabindranath Tagore, 1861–1941

Christian

In difficult times

Lord Jesus, kind heart,
Through the storms of the day
Guide me to the shore.
Lord Jesus, kind heart,
When darkness comes over me,
Give me your light.
Lord Jesus, kind heart,
I am weary with travelling,
Let me rest in you.

W. Mary Calvert

Christian

When tired or in need of rest

Good Jesus, strength of the weary, rest of the
   restless, by the weariness and unrest of your
   sacred cross, come to me who am weary
   that I may rest in you.

Edward Pusey, 1800–82

Christian

At a time of celebration

Our Lord,
Let us take this quiet moment to say a special
    word about the good things and the joy
    You have brought into our family.
Let us say it now with all our heart.
Thank you, Our Lord.
Amen.

Jewish

Blessing for caregivers

May the One who blessed our ancestors be
present to those who provide help for the ill
and troubled among us.
May they be filled with fortitude and courage,
And endowed with sympathy and compassion,
as they give strength to those at their side.
May they fight against despair, and continue
to find within themselves the will to reach
out to those in need.
And in their love of others, may they know
the blessing of community, and the blessing
of renewed faith.

Christian

A blessing for the family

Mary, Mother of Our Lord,
From your own experience,
    you share and understand ours.
Our Lady of Providence,
Queen of our Home,
We ask that your Holy Family bless
    and protect our family in all the
    days and nights to come.
Amen.

Christian

Needing to trust in God

Whether I fly with angels, fall with dust,
Thy hands made both, and I am there;
Thy power and love, my love and trust
Make one place everywhere.

George Herbert, 1593–1633

Christian

Fear or anxiety

In the hour of my fear I will put my trust in
you;
In God, whose word I praise, in God I trust
and will fear not;
What can flesh do to me?

Psalm 56: 3–4

Christian

In times of difficulty

My God, I can do no more!
Be for me the one who can!

Madame Acarie, 1566–1618

Hindu

Prayer for peace

Adorable Presence!

Thou who art within and without, above and
below and all around.

Thou who art interpreting the very cells of our
being.

Thou who art the Eye of our eyes, the Ear of
our ears, the Heart of our hearts, the Mind
of our minds, the Breath of our breaths, the
Life of our lives, and the Soul of our souls.

Bless us Dear God, to be aware of Thy
Presence here and now.

May all be aware of Thy Presence in the East
and the West, and the North and the
South;

May Peace and Goodwill abide among
individuals and also among communities
and nations.

This is our earnest prayer.

May peace be unto all.

Om Shanti! Peace! Shalom!

Christian

When ill

Heal me, O Lord, and I shall be healed; save
me and I shall be saved; for you are my
praise.

Jeremiah 17: 14

Islamic

Evening prayer

O God!
I go to sleep, awaken, live and die by you
and to you is the final gathering.
I go to sleep and the evening has come
with the Dominion belonging to God.
All praise is due to God, there is no partner
with Him, there is none worthy of worship
besides Him, and to Him is the final
gathering.

Prophet Mohammed, 570–632,
Founder of Islam

Hindu

Prayer for success

O Supreme Lord, may eminent scholars,
   possessing spiritual knowledge, be born in
   the state.
May valorous warriors, fit to rule, and expert
   archers, be born in the state.
May there be milky cows, stout oxen and swift
   horses.
May there be valiant women, heroic youths
   and victorious charioteers with the will to
   fight and fit to shine in assemblies.
May clouds shower rain, as profusely as we
   wish.
May our herbs and plants ripen and bear fruits
   in time.
May our joys be secure, under thy auspices.

Yajur Veda

Christian

For the sick

Bless the Lord, O my soul, let all that is
   within me bless his holy name; for he
   forgives all your sin and heals all your
   diseases.

Psalm 103: 1, 3

Christian

To live peacefully

O God, make us children of quietness,
   and heirs of peace.

St Clement of Alexandria, c. 150–215

Christian

Personal relationships

Almighty God,
Have mercy on all who bear me evil will and
    would harm me,
Forgive their faults and mine together;
Amend and redress and make us saved souls in
    heaven together,
Where we may ever live and love
Together with you and your blessed saints,
O glorious Trinity,
through the bitter passion of our sweet
    Saviour.

St Thomas More, 1478–1535

Christian

Grace for a special meal

Loving God,
We thank you for all our family and friends,
    elders and children,
For our loved ones to share the good times
    and the hard times, and the freedom to
    make of our lives what we choose.
At this special meal, we thank you for the gift
    of life and we remember those who still
    hunger and thirst.
We ask your continued blessings for them and
    for all whose love we share.
Amen.

Bahá'í

Prayer to be strong in times of hardship

Praise be unto Thee, O Lord.
Forgive us our sins, have mercy upon us and
    enable us to return unto Thee.
Suffer us not to rely on anything else besides
    Thee,
and vouchsafe unto us, through Thy bounty,
    that which Thou loves and desires.
Exalt the station of them that have truly
    believed, and forgive them with Thy
    gracious forgiveness.
Thou art the help in peril, the self-subsisting.

Abdu'l-Bahá, 1844–1921

Christian

For those who have died

Welcome, Lord, into your calm and peaceful
    kingdom those who, out of this present life,
    have departed to be with you.
Grant them rest and a place with the spirits of
    the just; and give them the life that knows
    not age, the reward that passes not away;
    through Jesus Christ our Lord.

St Ignatius of Loyola, 1491–1556

Christian

Faith in God

Like weary waves,
Thought flows upon thought,
But the still depth beneath
Is all thine own.

Père Grou, 1731–1803

Christian

Peacefulness

Drop thy still dews of quietness,
Till all our strivings cease;
Take from our souls the strain and stress,
And let our ordered lives confess
The beauty of thy peace.

John Greenleaf Whittier, 1807–1892

Christian

Morning prayer

Let this day, O Lord, add some knowledge or
good deed to yesterday.

Lancelot Andrews, 1555–1626

Hindu

Prayer for safety

O God, lead us from the unreal to the real.
O God, lead us from darkness to light.
O God, lead us from death to immortality.
O Lord God almighty,
And may your peace itself bestow peace on all,
and may that peace come to me also.

Christian

Blessing for food

Bless, O Lord, this food to our use
And ourselves to your service,
And make us mindful of the needs of others;
For your love's sake.

Christian

Before bed

Glory to thee, my God, this night
For all the blessings of the light;
Keep me, O keep me, King of kings,
Beneath thine own almighty wings.

Thomas Ken, 1637–1711

American Indian

Prayer for peace

Let us know peace.
For as long as the moon shall rise,
For as long as the rivers shall flow,
For as long as the sun shall shine,
For as long as the grass shall grow,
Let us know peace.

Hindu

A daily prayer

O gods!
All your names and forms are to be revered,
   saluted, and adored;
All of you who have sprung from heaven, and
   earth, listen here to my invocation.

Rig Veda X: 63: 2

Christian

Blessing for parents

May the Lord bless you all the days of your
    life;
May you see your children's children,
And in your home and country let there be
    peace.

Celtic

Faith

I am serene because I know thou lovest me.
Because thou lovest me, naught can move me
    from my peace.
Because thou lovest me, I am one to whom all
    good has come.

Ancient Celtic prayer

Christian

At a time of family crisis

Mary Mother of Our Lord,
Our family is straining.
We ask for your wisdom.
Help bring us back together and give us the
    strength to hold our tongues.
We trust in you, Our Lord. Light us the way
    to peace.
Amen.

Jewish

Prayer at time of trouble

God is our refuge and strength, a tested help
    in times of trouble.
Let the oceans roar and foam; let the
    mountains tremble.
There is a river of joy flowing through the
    City of our God, God himself is living in
    that City; therefore it stands unmoved
    despite the turmoil everywhere.
He will not delay his help.
The nations rant and rave in anger but when
    God speaks, the earth melts in submission
    and kingdoms totter into ruin.
The Commander of the armies of heaven is
    here among us. He, the God of Jacob, has
    come to rescue us.
Amen.

Psalm 46

Shamanistic

Praise for the gift of life

To our Mother Earth –
Thank you for the gifts of all creation.
From your body you give us the food we eat,
    the water we drink, the clothes we wear and
    the shelter of our homes.
You give us teachings of how to live upon you
    with harmony and balance.
You give us medicine when we are out of
    balance.
Thank you for your healing energy.
I pray for your health and healing and pray
    that your sacred waters, body, air and spirit
    will be clean and fresh, pure and strong.
With your help, may it be so.

Jewish

Healing prayer

God, hear my prayer,
And let my cry come to You.
Do not hide from me in the day of my distress
Turn to me and speedily answer my prayer.
Eternal God, source of healing,
Out of my distress I call upon You.
Help me sense Your presence
At this difficult time.
Grant me patience when the hours are heavy;
In hurt or disappointment give me courage.
Keep me trustful in Your love.
Give me strength for today, and hope for
    tomorrow.
To your loving hands I commit my spirit
When asleep and when awake. You are with
    me; I shall not fear.

Christian

Prayer for the family

Lord God, from you every family
in heaven and on earth takes its name.

Father, you are Love and Life.
Through your Son, Jesus Christ, born of
woman, and through the Holy Spirit,
fountain of divine charity, grant that every
family on Earth may become for each
successive generation a true shrine of life
and love.

Grant that your grace may guide the thoughts
and actions of husbands and wives for the
good of their families and of all the families
in the world.

Grant that the young may find in the family
solid support for their human dignity
and for their growth in truth and love.

Grant that love, strengthened by the grace of
the sacrament of marriage, may prove
mightier than all the weakness and trials
through which our families sometimes pass.

Through the intercession of the Holy Family
of Nazareth, grant that the Church may
fruitfully carry out her worldwide mission
in the family and through the family.

Through Christ our Lord, who is the Way, the
Truth and the Life for ever and ever.
Amen.

Pope John Paul II

Christian

When in fear

Hear my prayer, O God, and do not hide
 yourself from my petition; the terrors of
 death and trembling have come upon me,
 and horror overwhelms me.

Psalm 55: 1, 5

Christian

Prayer for a new school year

God, bless this family
 as we begin a new school year.
Let our home be a place to learn forgiveness,
 compassion, co-operation and
 responsibility.
Through Jesus Christ, your Son and Our
 Lord.
Amen.

Hindu

Prayer for peace

May there be peace in heaven.
May there be peace in the skies.
May there be peace on Earth,
   may there be peace in the waters.
May there be peace in the plants,
   may there be peace in the trees.
May we find peace in all the divining powers,
   may we find peace in the supreme Lord.
May we all be in peace
   and may that peace be mine.

The Hindu Vedas

Hindu

Morning prayer

Sun, anger, and the deities presiding over
    anger, save me from the sin committed
    through anger.
What sin I did at night, by mind, word and
    hands, by feet, stomach, or the organ of sex,
    may the deity presiding over the night
    destroy it.
Whatever remains in me as sin, that and my
    own self here, I am offering as an oblation
    in the light of the sun, the source of
    immortality.

Taittiriya Aranyaka X: 35

Buddhist

Morning prayer

Full of equanimity;
Of benevolent thought,
Of tender thought,
Of affectionate thought,
Of useful thought,
Of serene thought,
Of firm thought,
Of unbiased thought,
Of undisturbed thought,
Of unagitated thought,
Having entered on knowledge which is a firm
    support to all thoughts,
Equal to the ocean in wisdom,
Equal to the mountain Meru in knowledge,
Rich in many good qualities . . .
They attain perfect wisdom.

From the Sukhavativyuha Sutra

Hindu

Prayer for peace

Let there be peace in heaven.
Let there be peace in the atmosphere.
May the waters and medical herbs bring peace;
    may planets give peace to all beings.
May enlightened persons disseminate peace to
    all beings; and may that peace come to us
    and remain with us forever.

Yajur Veda

Christian

All saints

To all saints – ordinary people who helped in
    extraordinary ways.
They faced many obstacles and made changes
    in their lives to follow Jesus.
Our God, help us follow their example in our
    family life and in our contact with others.
We ask this in the name of Jesus Christ Our
    Lord.
Amen.

Shamanistic

For faith and trust

To the Power of the South, Power of faith and
   trust.
Help me, for I am weak and nothing without
   you.
Help me to surrender to your loving presence
   as the newly born infant trusts its parents.
Help me to shed the old trusting where new
   growth is already on its way.
I give thanks to you and pray for the
   strengthening of my faith in your always
   present presence.
With your help, may it be so.

Buddhist

Thanksgiving prayer

May the lamp of love which eternally burns
   above kindle divine fire in our hearts, and
   fan that innate spark of divinity into
   flame – illumining all, opening our eyes
   and consuming our differences, driving the
   shadows from our faces.
As love dawns on the horizon, may our
   community awaken in the kingdom of true
   communion, which is at hand always.
May we learn to love one another better even
   than we love ourselves.
God is great – may His grace be made
   manifest.
Love is stronger than death,
Yes.
Amen.

Lama Surya Das

Christian

Praise and thanksgiving

For the beauty of the earth,
For the beauty of the skies,
For the love which from our birth
Over and around us lies,
Lord of all, to Thee we raise
This our grateful hymn of praise.

For the beauty of each hour
Of the day and of the night,
Hill and vale, and tree and flower,
Sun and moon and stars of light,
Lord of all, to thee we raise
This our grateful hymn of praise.

Folliott S. Pierpoint, 1835–1917, adapted

Christian

An advent prayer

Lord in heaven, increase our longing for
    Christ, our Savior.
Give us the strength to grow in love, so that
    the dawn of his coming may find us
    rejoicing in his presence and welcoming the
    light of his truth.
We ask this in the name of Jesus Our Lord.
Amen.

Christian

Asking for help

Lead kindly light, amid the encircling gloom,
Lead Thou me on;
The night is dark, and I am far from home;
Lead thou me on.
Keep thou my feet; I do not ask to see
The distant scene – one step enough for me.

John Henry Newman, 1801–90

Hindu

Prayer for strength

Strike, strike at the root of penury in my
    heart.
Give me the strength lightly to bear my joys
    and sorrows.
Give me the strength to make my love fruitful
    in service.
Give me the strength never to disown the poor
    or bend my knees before insolence.
Give me the strength to raise my mind high
    above daily trifle.
And give me the strength to surrender my
    strength to thy will with love.

Rabindranath Tagore, 1861–1941

Christian

In hard times

Though I walk in the shadow of the valley of
death, I will fear no evil, for you are with
me, your rod and your staff comfort me.

Psalm 23: 4

Hindu

Prayer for peace

May all be happy.
May all be free from disease.
May all realize what is good.
May none be subject to misery.
Peace, Peace, Peace Be Unto All!

Ancient Hindu scriptures

Hindu

To the dawn

Listen to the salutation to the dawn,
Look to this day for it is life, the very life of
   life,
In its brief course lie all the verities and
   realities of our existence.
The bliss of growth, the splendor of beauty,
For yesterday is but a dream and tomorrow is
   only a vision,
But today well spent makes every yesterday a
   dream of happiness and every tomorrow a
   vision of hope.
Look well therefore to this day.
Such is the salutation to the dawn.

Sanskrit salutation

Hindu

Prayer for the unity of all life

May the winds, the oceans, the herbs, and
   night and days, the mother earth, the father
   heaven, all vegetation, the sun, be all sweet
   to us.
Let us follow the path of goodness for all
   times, like the sun and the moon moving
   eternally in the sky.
Let us be charitable to one another. Let us not
   kill or be violent with one another.
Let us know and appreciate the points of view
   of others. And let us unite.
May the God who is friendly, benevolent, all-
   encompassing, measurer of everything, the
   sovereign, the lord of speech, may He
   shower His blessings on us.
Oh Lord, remove my indiscretion and
   arrogance, control my mind. Put an end to
   the snare of endless desires. Broaden the
   sphere of compassion and help me to cross
   the ocean of existence.

Hindu

Divine blessing

Almighty Lord, if we offer you a devoted mind
and heart, you will offer to us every blessing
on earth and in heaven.

You grant our deepest wishes. You give food
to the body and peace to the soul. You look
upon us with the love of a mother for her
children.

You created this beautiful earth all around us.
And in every plant and animal, every tree
and bird, your spirit dwells.

You have revealed yourself to me, infusing my
soul with the knowledge that you are the
source of all blessing.

And so I sing your praises day and night. I
who am feeble, glorify you who are
powerful. I who am nothing, devote myself
to you who are everything.

Atharva Veda, c. 1,500 BC

Hindu

For peace

May the earth be free from disturbance,
May the vast atmosphere be calm,
May the flowing waters be soothing,
And all the plants and herbs prove beneficial
    to us.
May all the foretelling signs of coming events
    be free from turmoil and
May all that has been done and that which has
    not been done prove the source of
    happiness to all.
May our past and future be peaceful and may
    all be gracious unto us.
May the atmosphere be peaceful,
May the medicinal herbs be peaceful,
May all my shining objects be peaceful for me,
May all enlightened persons be peaceful for
    me,
May all the peaceful actions be peaceful by
    me.

Atharva Veda XIX: 9: 2

Christian

In times of difficulty

O Lord,
I cannot fight this dark with just my hands.
Help me to bring the light of Jesus into it.
Amen.

Christian

For faith

Lord, teach me to seek you,
And reveal yourself to me as I look for you.
For I cannot seek you unless first you reach
    me,
Nor find you unless first you reveal yourself to
    me.

St Ambrose, 340–397

Christian

Prayer for forgiveness

Lord, you know well that I love you;
Have pity on me, for I am nothing but a sinner.

St Therese of Lisieux, 1873–97

Hindu

Blessings

May your counsel be common,
May you belong to one fraternity,
May your minds move, with one accord.
May your hearts work in harmony for one goal.
May you be inspired, by common ideal.
May you offer worship, with common
     oblation.
May you resolve, with one accord.
May your hearts be in unison.
May your thoughts be harmonious,
So that you live together with happiness and
     hilarity.

Rig Veda X: 191: 3–4

Hindu

Prayer for forgiveness

Whatever sins have been committed by me, in
    thought, word or deed,
May the Supreme Lord, source of all strength,
    wisdom and purity, forgive me and purify
    me of them all.
May my body become pure.
May I be free from impurity and sin.
May I realize myself as the light divine.
May my mind become ever pure.
May my self become pure.
May I realize my self as the light divine.

Yajur Veda

Buddhist

Blessing and healing

Just as the soft rains fill the streams, pour into
the rivers and join together in the oceans,
so may the power of every moment of your
goodness flow forth to awaken and heal all
beings:
Those here now, those gone before, those yet
to come.
By the power of every moment of your
goodness may your heart's wishes be soon
fulfilled as completely shining as the bright
full moon, as magically as by a wish-
fulfilling gem.
By the power of every moment of your
goodness may all dangers be averted and all
disease gone.
May no obstacle come across your way;
may you enjoy fulfilment and long life.
For all in whose heart dwells respect,
follow the wisdom and compassion of the
Way.
May your life prosper in the four blessings of
old age, beauty, happiness and strength.

Christian

Morning prayer

Lord, I my vows to Thee renew,
Please scatter my sins as morning dew;
Guard my first springs of thought and will,
And with Thyself my spirit fill.

Thomas Ken, 1637–1711

Jewish

A prayer for peace

Come let us go up to the mountain of the
    Lord, that we may walk the paths of the
    Most High.
And we shall beat our swords into plowshares,
    and our spears into pruning hooks.
Nation shall not lift up sword against nation –
    neither shall they learn war any more.
And none shall be afraid, for the mouth of the
    Lord of Hosts has spoken.
Amen.

Hindu

Prayer to grow hair

Born from the bosom of wide Earth art thou:
So we dig thee up to strengthen and fix fast
    the hair.
Make the old firm, make new hair grow and
    lengthen what has already grown.

Atharva Veda VI: 22

Christian

Before bed

While I sleep, O Lord,
Let my heart not cease to worship you;
Fill my sleep with your presence,
While creation itself keeps watch,
Singing psalms with the angels,
And taking up my soul into its paean of
    praise.

St Gregory of Nazianzus, c. 330–89

Hindu

Prayer at cremation
(to the deceased)

Let your eye go to the sun, your life to the
    wind.
By the meritorious acts that you have done, go
    to heaven, and then to the earth again;
Or, resort to the waters, if you feel at home
    there; remain in the herbs with the bodies
    you propose to take.

Rig Veda X: 16: 3

Christian

Praise and thanksgiving

I thank you, O God, for the pleasures you
    have given me through my senses;
For the glory of thunder and the mystery of
    music;
For the singing of birds and laughter of
    children.
I thank you for the delights of colour, the awe
    of the sunset, the wild roses in the
    hedgerows, the smile of friendship.
I thank you for the sweetness of the flowers
    and the scent of hay.
Truly, O Lord, the earth is full of your riches.

Edward King, 1829–1910, adapted

Bahá'í

Prayer to be free of anxiety

O God! Refresh and gladden my spirit.
Purify my heart.
Illumine my powers.
I lay all my affairs in Thy hand.
Thou art my Guide and my Refuge.
I will no longer be sorrowful and grieved;
I will be a happy and joyful being.
O God! I will no longer be full of anxiety,
    nor will I let trouble harass me.
I will not dwell on the unpleasant things of
    life.
O God! Thou art more friend to me than I am
    to myself.
I dedicate myself to Thee, O Lord.

Abdu'l-Bahá, 1844–1921

Hindu

Prayer for desire

Desire did it,
Desire does it,
I do not do it.
Desire is the doer,
I am not the doer.
Desire is the agent,
I am not the agent.
O Desire, here, this oblation to you!

Taittiriya Aranyaka X: 41–42

Christian

For when you are moving house

Lord help me in this move.
Help me to keep my many memories,
    from this familiar place.
To Our Lord who never changes.
Help me to remember Thy constant blessing.
Amen.

Islamic

Daily prayer

Praise be to the cherisher and sustainer of the
    Worlds.
Most gracious, most merciful,
Master of the day of judgement.
Thee do we worship and Thine aid we seek.
Show us the straight way:
the way of those on whom Thou hast
    bestowed Thy grace,
Those whose portion is not wrath
And who go not astray.

Sura Fatiha, The Lord's Prayer

Islamic

Prayer for peace

Oh God,
You are Peace.
From You comes Peace,
To You returns Peace.
Revive us with a salutation of Peace,
And lead us to your abode of Peace.

Sikh

Prayer of repentance

Our transgressions are past counting,
There is no end to our sins,
Be merciful, forgive us, O Lord;
We are great sinners and wrongdoers.
There is no hope of our redemption.
O Lord, dear Lord, our deeds weighed in the
   balance would get us no place in Thy court!
Forgive us and make us one with Thyself
Through the grace of the Guru.
If the Lord God can be attained to,
Then all evil is destroyed.

Christian

Prayer for a new year

Our Lord God,
A new year is beginning, let it remind us of
    our place in time.
We are part of this world you made,
Our strength comes from your mountains,
Our patience from your lakes, and
Our love from our brothers and sisters
With whom we share this world.

Let us face this year with the blessing to do
    better in all we do.
Help us to better understand our part in your
    creation.
Help us to make this world a better place, now
    and forever.
Amen.

Islamic

Our trust

Lord, in you we put our trust.
To you we turn in times of need.
To you we shall go at the moment of death.
Do not allow us to be deceived and misled
by the designs of those whose hearts are evil.
Forgive us for the evil in our own hearts.
You alone are mighty; you alone are wise.

Prophet Mohammed, 570–632,
Founder of Islam

Christian

For the sick

Dear God,
Through your infinite love and power
May release from all sickness and infirmity
  be given to those for whom we pray.

Shamanistic

For a birth

To our Creator, at the center of all things, all
   times, all persons, all places, and who have
   always been and will be always.
Thank you for this precious breath of life.
Thank you for the Gifts of Creation.
Thank you for this day and the opportunity to
   know, love and serve you.
Thank you for the gifts of our families, our
   teachers, our ancestors, and those we are
   ancestors for.
Thank you for the beauty and power that lives
   beneath our feet in our dear Mother Earth.
Thank you for the abundance of life.
Thank you for the food and water.
Let us listen to your deep intelligence guiding
   us to harmony and balance with your help
   and the help of all our relations,
With your help, may it be so.

Islamic

Prayer for peace

Praise be to the Lord of the Universe who has
created us and made us into tribes and
nations, so that we may know each other,
not that we may despise each other.
If the enemy incline towards peace, do thou
also incline towards peace, and trust in
God, for the Lord is the one that heareth
and knoweth all things.
And the servants of God, most gracious are
those who walk on the earth in humility, and
when we address them, we say, "Peace."

Shintoist

Prayer for peace

Why are there constant troubles in this world?
Why do winds and waves rise in the ocean
surrounding us?
I only earnestly wish that the wind will puff
away all the clouds hanging over the tops of
the mountains.

Jainist

Prayer for peace

Lead me from Death to Life, from Falsehood
to Truth.
Lead me from Despair to Hope, from Fear to
Trust.
Lead me from Hate to Love, from War to
Peace.
Let Peace fill our Hearts, our World, our
Universe.

Islamic

For help and guidance

O my Lord! Grant me that I may be grateful
for Thy favour which Thou has bestowed
upon me;
And also upon both my parents,
that I may work righteousness such as Thou
may approve.
Be gracious to me in my issue.
Truly have I turned to Thee and truly do I
bow to Thee in Islam.

Surah 46: Al-Ahqaf (The Dunes): 15

Sikh

Prayer for abundance

May the kingdom of justice prevail!
May the believers be united in love!
May the hearts of the believers be humble,
    high their wisdom,
And may they be guided in their wisdom by
    the Lord.
Glory be to God!
Entrust unto the Lord what thou wishest to be
    accomplished.
The Lord will bring all matters to fulfilment.
Know this as truth evidenced by Himself.

Bahá'í

Prayer for guidance

Be generous in prosperity, and thankful in
    adversity.
Be fair in your judgment, and guarded in your
    speech.
Be a lamp unto those who walk in darkness,
    and a home to the stranger.
Be eyes to the blind, and a guiding light unto
    the feet of the erring.
Be a breath of life to the body of humankind,
    a dew to the soil of the human heart, and a
    fruit upon the tree of humility.

Islamic

To be granted a son

O my Lord!
Grant me a righteous son.

Surah 37: As-Saaffat
(Drawn Up In Ranks): 100

Christian

A prayer for Father's Day

St Joseph,
Through your goodness, faith and quiet
   sacrifice, you taught the meaning of
   fatherhood.
You offered us guidance and you showed the
   way.
Thank you for those who brought fatherhood
   into my life, especially my own father.
I turn to you today, and seek blessings for my
   father and for all good men who have
   touched my life.

Christian

For freedom from addictions

Our Lord Jesus in Heaven,
One we love is bound by addictions.
We pray for him/her because addictions end
    choices.
You died, Lord, to make us free to choose our
    destiny.
Please, Lord, help one we love break free of
    addiction and, in his/her freedom walk
    back to us and to you.
Amen.

Christian

For a strengthening of faith
for a family member

Faith is not always a constant.
Our family has become troubled.
We ask your help so that our loved ones can
    find the simple and quiet path back to you.
Amen.

American Indian

A prayer for peace

O Great Spirit of our ancestors, I raise my
pipe to you.
To your messengers the four winds, and to
Mother Earth who provides for your
children: give us the wisdom to teach our
children to love, to respect and to be kind
to each other so that they may grow with
peace in mind.
Let us learn to share all the good things that
you provide for us on this Earth.

Christian

For harmony among people

O God of peace, good beyond all that is good,
in whom is calmness and concord:
Heal the dissensions which divide us from one
another, and bring us into unity of love for
you; through Jesus Christ our Lord.

St Dionysius of Alexandria, c. 190–265

Christian

Night-time prayer

Watch, dear Lord, with those who wake or
weep tonight, and let your angels protect
those who sleep.
Tend the sick; refresh the weary; sustain the
dying; calm the suffering; pity the
distressed.
We ask this for your love's sake.

St Augustine of Hippo, 354–430

Shamanistic

Thankful for light

To Father Sky, Father Sun and Grandmother
Moon.
Thank you for your light and your love, your
company through day and night.
Thank you for the gifts of rain that come to
quench our Mother's thirst.
Help me to open myself to your teachings of
balanced energies.
I give thanks to all you who are above and
thank you for your gifts of vision.
With your help, may it be so.

American Indian

Prayer giving thanks for all life

Great and Eternal Mystery of Life, Creator of
   All Things, I give thanks for the beauty You
   put in every single one of Your creations.
I am grateful that You did not fail in making
   every stone, plant, creature, and human
   being a perfect and whole part of the Sacred
   Hoop.
I am grateful that You have allowed me to see
   the strength and beauty of all my relations.
My humble request is that all of the children
   of Earth will learn to see the same
   perfection in themselves.
May none of Your human children doubt or
   question Your wisdom, grace, and sense of
   wholeness in giving all of Creation a right
   to be living extensions of Your perfect love.

Inuit

Prayer at time of adversity

I think over again my small adventures and
    my fears.
Those small ones that seemed so big, for all
    the vital things I had to get and reach.
And yet there is only one great thing,
The only thing,
To live to see the great day that dawns, and
    the light that fills the world.

African

Prayer for peace

Almighty God, the Great Thumb we cannot
    evade which ties any knot; the roaring
    Thunder that splits mighty trees: the all-
    seeing Lord up on high who sees even the
    footprints of antelope on a rock mass here
    on Earth.
You are the one who does not hesitate to
    respond to our call.
You are the cornerstone of peace.

Ashanti (Ghanaian)

Prayer for blessing

O Lord, O God, creator of our land, our
earth, the trees, the animals and humans, all
is for your honor.
Bless us.
Bless our land and people.
Bless our forests with mahogany, and cacao.
Bless our fields with cassava and peanuts.
Bless the waters that flow through our land.
Fill them with fish and drive great schools of
fish to our sea coast, so that the fishermen
in their unsteady boats do not need to go
out too far.
Be with us youth in our countries, and in all
Africa, and in the whole world.
Prepare us for the service that we should
render.

Sikh

Prayer for humility

There is no counting the number of fools,
No counting the thieves and fraudsters,
No counting those who shed innocent blood,
No counting the adulterers and the traitors,
No counting the liars who take pleasure in
    deceit,
No counting those who spread malice and
    hatred.
I do not put myself above any of those people,
I am the lowliest of the low.
I have nothing to offer you, O Lord.
My life is not even worth sacrificing to you.
All I can do is try to obey your will.
All I want is to abide in your peace.

Guru Nanak, 1469–1538,
Founder of the Sikh religion

Bahá'í

A healing prayer

Thy name is my healing, O my God,
and remembrance of Thee is my remedy.
Nearness to Thee is my hope
and love for Thee is my companion.
Thy mercy to me is my healing and my succor
    in both this world and the world to come.
Thou, art the All-Bountiful, the All-Knowing,
    the All-Wise.
Say: God knows all things above all things;
    and nothing in the heavens or on the earth
    but God knows.
He is in Himself the Knowledge, the
    Sustainer, the Omnipotent.

Hindu

Prayer for protection

O all powerful God,
Thou art the protector of the whole physical
    creation.
May Thou protect my body.
Thou art the source of all life.
Thou art the source of all strength, may thou
    make me strong.
O, omnipotent Lord, I live to thee to fill up
    all my wants and give me perfection,
    physical, mental and spiritual.

Kenyan (Samburu)

Prayer to give thanks

Thank you very, very much;
My God, thank you.
Give me food today,
Food for my sustenance every day.
Thank you very, very much.

Bahá'í

Prayer for assistance in difficult times

O Lord! Thou art the remover of all anguish
   and the deliverer from every affliction.
Thou art He who banishes every sorrow and
   sets free every slave, the redeemer of every
   soul.
O Lord! Grant deliverance through Thy
   mercy; and reckon me among such servants
   of Thine as have gained salvation.

Abdu'l-Bahá, 1844–1921

American Indian

Sioux prayer

O our Father, the Sky, hear us
    and make us strong.
O our Mother the Earth, hear us
    and give us support.
O Spirit of the East,
    send us your Wisdom.
O Spirit of the South,
    may we tread your path of life.
O Spirit of the West,
    may we always be ready for the long journey.
O Spirit of the North, purify us
    with your cleansing winds.

Christian

For guidance

O! Thou that are manifest, be Thou manifest
    to us:
From the unreal lead us to real,
From darkness lead us to light,
From death lead us to immortality!

Shamanistic

For all relatives

Thank you for our ancestors going back to the
   very beginning.
And thank you for grandparents and for
   intimate life partners such as wives and
   husbands.
Thank you for our gift of sisters and brothers,
   for aunts and uncles, for cousins, nieces and
   nephews.
Thank you for all those who nourish and
   protect our place on this earth
With your help, may it be so.

Christian

For conflict resolution

Dear God,
When your son
Our Lord Jesus died and rose from the dead,
    he broke down walls of hostility.
Please help me in this conflict.
Help me to follow in your righteous path.
For you are Our Lord God and Savior.
Amen.

Inuit (West Greenland)

Prayer for newborn girl

That she was taken out of her mother,
Thanks be for that!
That she, the little one, was taken out of her,
    we say,
Thanks be for that!

Christian

Thanksgiving at mealtimes

O Great Spirit, Creator and source of every
   blessing, we pray that you will bring peace
   to all our brothers and sisters of this world.
Give us wisdom to teach our children to love,
   to respect and to be kind to each other.
Help us to learn to share all the good things
   that you provide for us.
Bless all those who share this meal with us
   today.
We ask your special blessing on those who are
   hungry today, especially little children.
Help us to be just and to bring your peace to
   all the earth.
Praise and thanksgiving be to you.

Christian

Prayer to do God's will

Dearest Lord, teach me to be generous;
Teach me to serve thee as thou deserves;
To give and not to count the cost,
To fight and not to seek for rest,
To labour and not to seek reward,
Save that of knowing that I do thy will.

St Ignatius of Loyola, 1491–1556

Christian

Prayer for diverse blessings

In mercy you have seen fit today to show me,
    poor as I am, how we can in no way pass
    judgment on other people's intentions.
Indeed, by sending people along an endless
    variety of paths, you give me an example for
    myself, and for this I thank you.

St Catherine of Siena, 1347–1380

Christian

A prayer for expectant mothers

Most Gracious Heavenly Father,
We thank You for our mothers to whom You
   have entrusted the care of all precious
   human life from its very beginning.
Watch over every mother who is with child,
   strengthen her faith in Your fatherly care
   and love for her and for her unborn baby.
Give her courage in times of fear or pain,
   understanding in times of uncertainty and
   doubt, and hope in times of trouble.
Grant her joy in the birth of her child.
Amen.

Jewish

Prayer after meals

We give thanks for all your gifts,
Almighty God, who lives and reigns forever.
May the souls of the faithful departed,
    through the mercy of God, rest in peace.
Amen.

Christian

A child's prayer for parents

Heavenly Father, I thank you for my father
    and mother, and for our home.
Bless us all, and help us to love you and in
    love to serve one another as Jesus taught us
    to do.
Give me strength to do what is right today,
    and to do to others as I would want them
    to do to me.
Amen.

Christian

Thanks for father

I thank you, Lord, for my father.
Help me to realize the depth of his love for me
and appreciate his great and continuous
sacrifices.
His fatherly care reflects your divine care; his
strength, your power; his understanding,
your wisdom.
He is your faithful servant and image.
Bless him with peace of soul, health of body,
and success in his life.
Amen.

Hindu

On being pleased for another's good fortune

When a person responds to the joys and
sorrows of others as if they were his own, he
has attained the highest state of spiritual
union.

The Bhagavad Gita 6:32, Sri Krishna

Christian

A father's prayer for loved ones

Kind Father,
I thank You for my home where loved ones
    dwell.
I praise You for the family love, peace and
    cheer which follow me and comfort me.
I am grateful for all things that bind us closer
    to each other.
Shelter my home. O God, and my dear ones
    there.
Make me strong, unselfish, and brave to
    defend and protect them.
Send down Your peace to every family on
    earth
and grant an abundance of grace to them.
May they merit the joys of eternal salvation.
Amen.

Christian

A prayer of parents for their children

Almighty God, you have called us to the holy
   state of matrimony and have shared with us
   your gift of creation.
We thank you for making our love fruitful.
May we be worthy representatives of you, dear
   Lord, in forming our children in your
   knowledge and love.
May our children ever walk in the way of your
   commandments and live according to the
   teachings of your Church.
May we be firm but kind in discipline.
May we stand as one, united in authority so as
   to be consistent.
May we teach our children respect for your
   authority in ourselves.
Amen.

Christian

Prayer of a worker

Lord, Jesus Christ,
I offer You today all my work, my hopes, my
   sorrows and joys.
Grant me the grace to remain close to You
   today, to work with You and to do all that I
   do for Your honor and glory.
Help me, Lord, to give a full day's work for a
   full day's pay.
Help me to respect the property of others and
   to be honest in dealing with those involved
   in this task. Give me the spirit of charity
   that I may contribute to the happiness of all
   those with whom I work, and when the job
   is done, grant us all a peaceful rest.
Saint Joseph, patron of workers, pray for me.

Jewish

For affirmation of faith

Hear, O Israel:
The Lord our God is one Lord:
And thou shalt love the Lord thy God with all
    thine heart,
and with all thy soul, and with all thy might.

Deuteronomy 6: 4–5

American Indian (Navajo)

The beautiful trail

With your feet, I walk.
I walk with your limbs.
I carry forth your body.
For me your mind thinks.
Your voice speaks for me.
Beauty is before me.
And beauty is behind me.
Above and below me hovers the beautiful.
I am surrounded by it.
I am immersed in it.
In my youth I am aware of it.
And in old age I shall walk quietly,
The beautiful trail.

Christian

A father's prayers of petition

As the guardian of my family I pray to the
Lord.
When I am discouraged and weary, give me
the grace to be strong.
Help me to be a source of patience,
understanding and love to my family.
Help me to teach my children always to do
Your will.
Help me willingly and joyfully to accept the
sacrifices I must make for the good of my
family.
Help me to instil in my children a love for Jesus
so that they may bear witness to others.

Sikh

Farewell blessing

May the long time sun
Shine upon you,
All love surround you,
And the pure light within you
Guide your way on.

Kundalini yoga

Jewish

To give thanks for the world

The earth is full of Your goodness,
Your greatness and understanding,
Your wisdom and harmony.
How wonderful are the lights that You
    created.
You formed them with strength and power
    and they shine very wonderfully on the
    world, magnificent in their splendor.
They arise in radiance and go down in joy.
Reverently they fulfill Your divine will.
They are tributes to Your name
as they exalt Your sovereign rule in song.

Mystical hymn, 516 BC

Jewish

Be still

Be still.
Know I am God.
I speak to you through the storm and the
    clouds.
Be still.
Know I am God.
I speak to you through the thunder and
    lightning.
Be still.
Know I am God.
I speak to you through the mysterious
    rainbow.
Be still.
Know I am God.
I will speak to you when you are alone.
Be still.
Know I am God.
I will speak to you through the Wisdom of the
    Ancients.
Be still.
Know I am God.
I will speak to you at the end of time.
Be still.
Know I am God.
I will speak to you when you have seen my
    angels.

Be still.
Know I am God.
I will speak to you throughout eternity.
Be still.
Know I am God.
I speak to you.
Be still.
Know I am God.

From the Essene Gospel of Peace

Christian

Prayer when ill

Lord allow Your healing hand to heal me.
Touch my soul with Your compassion.
Touch my heart with Your courage.
Touch my mind with Your wisdom.
Most loving Jesus, bring me health in body
   and spirit that I may serve You with all my
   strength.
Amen.

Sikh

Prayer of the soul

Pleasing God,
Is the only ritual I do,
Without inner experience
All rituals mean nothing.

Japji, Meditation of the Soul

Jewish

In difficult times

Hear my cry, O God;
    listen to my prayer.
From the ends of the earth I call to you.
I call as my heart grows faint;
    lead me to the rock that is higher than I.
For you have been my refuge,
    a strong tower against the foe.
I long to dwell in your tent forever
    and take refuge in the shelter of your wings.

Psalm of David, Psalms 61: 1–4

Hindu

Praise for the mystery of God

Indeed, You alone know Yourself
   by Your own potencies,
O origin of all,
Lord of all beings,
God of gods,
O Supreme Person,
Lord of the universe!

The Bhagavad Gita: 10: 15 – Arjuna

Jewish

For help and guidance

Cast me not away from thy presence;
    and take not thy Holy Spirit from me.
Restore unto me the joy of thy salvation;
    and uphold me with thy free spirit.

Psalms 51: 11–12

Hindu

Love and praise

That one I love is incapable of ill will,
He is friendly and compassionate.
Living beyond the reach of I and mine
    and of pleasure and pain.
Patient, contented, self-controlled,
    firm in faith, with all His heart and all of
    His mind given to me –
With such a one I am in love.

The Bhagavad Gita 12: 13–14 – Sri Krishna

Hindu

To God the Father

You are Father of the world,
Of animate and inanimate things;
Its venerable teacher,
Most worthy of worship,
Without equal.
Where in all three worlds is another to match
   your extraordinary power?
I bow to you,
I prostrate my body,
I beg you to be a gracious worshipful Lord.
As a father to a son,
A friend to a friend,
A lover to a beloved,
O God, bear with me.

The Bhagavad Gita 11: 43–44 – Arjuna

Kundalini yoga

Prayer for the world

May the whole world enjoy
Good health,
Long life,
Prosperity,
Happiness and peace.

Kundalini yoga master, Vethathiri Maharishi

Hindu

For common unity

Let us be united;
Let us speak in harmony;
Let our minds apprehend alike.
Common be our prayer,
Common be the end of our assembly;
Common be our resolution;
Common be our deliberations.
Alike be our feelings;
Unified be our hearts;
Common be our intentions;
Perfect be our unity.

From the Rig Veda

Hindu

For peace

I desire neither earthly kingdom,
    nor even freedom from birth and death.
I desire only the deliverance from grief
    of all those afflicted by misery.
Oh Lord, lead us from the unreal to the real;
    from darkness to light;
    from death to immortality.
May there be peace in celestial regions.
May there be peace on Earth.
May the waters be appeasing.
May herbs be wholesome and may trees and
    plants bring peace to all.
May all beneficent beings bring peace to us.
May thy wisdom spread peace all through the
    world.
May all things be a source of peace to all and
    to me.

Sikh

God's purity

There is one, only one
With true identity
Who does it all
Has no fear
Or enmity
An eternal entity
Free from rebirths
A self-existent luminary
Attainable through
The grace of the Guru.

Jewish

For affirmation of belief

Wherever I go, only Thou
Wherever I stand, only Thou
Just Thou, again Thou
and always Thou
When things are good, Thou
When things are bad, Thou
Thou, Thou, Thou

Hasidic song

Christian

Prayer for husbands and wives

O Lord, inspire all those men and women
    who bear the titles Husband and Wife.
Help them to look to you, to themselves, and
    to one another.
Let them be honest enough to ask:
Where have we been together and where are
    we going?
Let them be brave enough to question:
How have we failed?
Let each be foolhardy enough to say:
For me, you come first.
Help them, together, to believe how powerful
    their love can be.
Amen.

Christian

Morning prayer

O Lord God,
May it please Thee this day to govern our
   hearts, our bodies, our thoughts, our words
   and our works, according to Thy law and in
   being helped by Thee, may here and
   hereafter be saved.
Amen.

*Office of Prime in the Roman Breviary, Ancient
Roman Christian*

Hindu

For peace

O Gods!
All your names and forms are to be revered,
   saluted and adored.
Oh Almighty! Life is oblation.
We offer all fruits of duty to you.
Kindly concede we surrender everything to
   you.
Oh Almighty! May there be a peace everywhere.

The Bhagavad Gita 4: 24

Sikh

God's benevolence

He speaks sweetly dear,
   that enlightening love of mine.
I'm exhausted having searched his words; he
   never speaks unkind.
He knows not foul language, the pure and
   perfect embodiment of the infinite; he lets
   my weaknesses go unrecorded.
The polluted ones, he makes pure, as is his
   nature.
Not one virtue does he leave without reward.
In each and every, and all, he dwells, nearest
   of the near.
That sublime, immortal, enlightening love of
   mine.

Sri Guru Granth Sahib, 1469

Christian

Blessing for the home

Visit, we beg Thee, O Lord, this dwelling, and
    drive from it all the snares of the enemy;
Let Thy holy angels dwell herein to keep us in
    peace;
And let Thy blessing be always upon us.
Amen.

Ancient Roman Christian

Christian

Confirmation of faith

O God, for you my soul is thirsting.
I long for you like dry, weary land without
    water.
Give me your strength and your glory.
I wish to praise you all my life
Hold me close in your hands.

Psalm 63

Christian

Bedtime prayer

Jesus Christ, my God, I adore Thee and thank
    Thee for all the graces Thou hast given me
    this day.
I offer Thee my sleep and all the moments of
    this night, and I beseech Thee to keep me
    without sin.
I put myself within Thy sacred side and under
    the mantle of our Lady, my mother.
Let Thy holy angels stand about me and keep
    me in peace;
And let Thy blessing be upon me.
Amen.

St Alphonsus Maria de Liguori, 1696–1787

Christian

Daily prayer

I lift my heart to you, O Lord,
    to be strengthened for this day.
Be with me in all I do
    and guide me in all my ways.
I will carry some burdens today;
    some trials will be mine.
So I ask for your help, O Lord,
    lest I stumble and fall.
I will do my work, Father,
    the work begun by your Son.
He lives in me and I in him;
    may his work today be done.
Amen.

Christian

Morning prayer

I call upon you, O Lord.
In the morning you hear me;
    in the morning I offer you
    my prayer, watching and waiting.

Psalm 5

Christian

Daily prayer

Into Thy hands, O Lord, into the hands of
Thy holy angels, I commit and entrust this
day my soul, my relations, my benefactors,
my friends and enemies.
Keep us, O Lord, through the day from all
vicious and unruly desires, from all sins and
temptations of the devil, and from sudden
and unprovided death and the pains of hell.
Illuminate my heart with the grace of Thy
Holy Spirit.
Grant that I may ever be obedient to Thy
commandments; and suffer me not to be
separated from Thee.
Amen.

St Edmund Rich,
Archbishop of Canterbury, 1180–1242

Christian

Affirmation of faith

Dear Father in heaven,
I lift my eyes to you and wait for your help.
I am your servant, entrusted with your gifts.
Like a faithful servant, I wish to do your
  bidding.
As the eyes of a good servant are on the
  master, so are our eyes on the Lord, our
  God, till he bless us.

Psalm 12

Christian

Morning prayer

Lord, teach us to number our days aright,
  that we may gain wisdom of heart.

Psalm 90

Christian

Morning

Sing joyfully to the Lord, all you lands;
  serve the Lord with gladness; come before
  him with joyful song.
Know that the Lord is God; he made us, his
  we are; his people, the flock he tends.
Enter his gates with thanksgiving, his courts
  with praise;
Give thanks to him; bless his name, for he is
  good: the Lord, whose kindness endures
  forever, and his faithfulness to all
  generations.

Psalm 100

156

Christian

Morning prayer

Help us do today the things that matter,
   not to waste the time we have.
Fill us this day with your kindness, that we may
   be glad and rejoice all the days of our life.

Christian

Evening

Lord, as this day ends, bless my soul and body
   for I am tired.
And is all I have done worthwhile?
I need you, Lord.
Help me to turn to you.
Amen.

Christian

Evening

The Lord is my light and my salvation,
  whom should I fear?
The Lord is my life's refuge; of whom should I
  be afraid?
Hear, O Lord, the sound of my call; have pity
  on me, and answer me.
Of you my heart speaks; of you my glance
  seeks.
Your presence, O Lord, this night I seek.

Psalm 27

Christian

Morning

Praise the Lord, my thoughts and deeds of this
 day.
I will praise the Lord wherever I go; for the
 Lord is good.

Christian

Thanks for a problem solved

Lord, I thank you for the many times you gave
 me help, always listening when I called.
In my darkest moments, when all seemed to
 be lost, there you were, at my side.
The Lord always listens and has pity;
 the Lord always comes to our help.
Our mourning you change into dancing;
 you always clothe us with joy.

Psalm 30

Christian

To start each day anew

Have mercy on me, O God, in your goodness;
   in the greatness of your compassion wipe
   out my offence.
Thoroughly wash me from my guilt and of my
   sin cleanse me, a steadfast spirit renew
   within me.
Cast me not out from your presence,
   cleanse me of sin that I may be purified;
   wash me, and I shall be whiter than snow.

Psalm 51

Christian

Evening thanks

My God, every day I praise you,
You are good and merciful, slow to anger and
of great kindness.
You are faithful in all Your words and holy in
all Your works.
You lift up all who are falling and raise up all
who are bowed down.
The eyes of all look hopefully to You, and You
give them their food in due season;
Open Your hand and satisfy the desire of every
living thing.

Psalm 145

Christian

In praise

Praise the Lord, all you nations, glorify God,
all you peoples!
For steadfast is God's kindness toward us
and the fidelity of the Lord endures forever.

Psalm 117

Christian

Daily prayer

Praise the Lord, faraway space, glorify God,
   every home and family.
For God has brought us to the beginning of
   this day, and God will see us to its end.
Praise the Lord, world of today, come with
   your blessings; come with your struggles.
Praise the Lord!
Amen.

Christian

Prayer for deliverance
from hard times

Out of my fears, failures and sins, I cry to you
    Lord, hear my voice.
Out of the depths of my heart I cry to you,
    from the darkness of myself.
Lord hear my voice.
For you are merciful Lord forgiving to us all.
Let Your mercy come as sure as the dawn.

Christian

Prayer before surgery

Loving Father, I entrust myself to your care on
    this day.
And pray that I may be restored to soundness
    of health and learn to live in more perfect
    harmony with you and with those around
    me.
Into your hands, I commend my body and my
    soul.
Amen.

Christian

Prayer for after surgery

Blessed Saviour, I thank you that the surgery is
   safely past, and now I rest in your abiding
   presence.
In moments of pain I turn to you for strength,
   in times of loneliness I feel your loving
   nearness.
Grant that your life and love and joy may flow
   through me.
Amen.

Christian

Prayer for medical staff

O merciful Father we pray for all those who
    heal the sick and prevent disease and pain.
Strengthen them in body and soul,
and bless their work, that they may give
    comfort.
Amen.

Christian

Prayer for the dying

Our Lord Jesus have mercy on the dying and
    grant that they may breathe forth their soul
    in peace with you.
Amen.

Christian

Prayer to maintain health

Into your most holy hands I commit the
keeping of my heart, asking you for health
of soul and body, in the hope that you will
hear my prayer.
Into the bosom of your tender mercy, this day
and every day of my life, I commend my
soul and body.
To you I entrust all my hopes and
consolations, all my trials and miseries, my
life and the end of my life.
Amen.

Jewish

A blessing

The Lord bless you and keep you;
The Lord make his face shine upon you and
    be gracious to you;
The Lord turn his face toward you and give
    you peace.

Numbers 6: 24–26

Christian

Prayer for healing

Lord, look upon me with eyes of mercy.
May your healing hand rest upon me.
May your life-giving powers flow into every
    cell of my body restoring me to wholeness
    and strength for Your service.
Amen.

Christian

Keeping the faith

Breathe in me, Holy Spirit, that I may think
what is holy.
Move me, Holy Spirit, that I may do what is
holy.
Attract me, Holy Spirit, that I may love what
is holy.
Strengthen me, Holy Spirit that I may guard
what is holy.
Guard me, Holy Spirit that I may keep what is
holy.

St Augustine of Hippo, 354–430

Christian

Prayer for the sick

Dear Jesus, Divine Physician and Healer of
   the sick, we turn to you in this time of
   illness.
Alleviate our worry and sorrow with your
   gentle love, and grant us the grace and
   strength to accept this burden.
Amen.

Christian

Blessing of a new house

Almighty God, we humbly beseech Thee to
   bless and sanctify this house and all who
   dwell therein and everything else in it.
At our entrance deign to bless and sanctify this
   house and may the angels of Thy light,
   dwelling within the walls of this house,
   protect it and those who dwell therein.
Amen.

Christian

Prayer for the sick

Tend your sick ones, O Lord.
Rest your weary ones.
Bless your dying ones.
Soothe your suffering ones.
Pity your afflicted ones.
Shield your joyous ones.
For all your love's sake.
Amen.

St Augustine of Hippo, 354–371

Christian

Night-time prayer

Watch, O Lord, with those who wake, or
    watch, or weep tonight,
and give your angels charge over those who
    sleep.

Christian

Prayer in time of trial

O good Jesus, I accept willingly this trial
    which it has pleased you to lay upon me.
I confide all my pains to your Sacred Heart,
    and beg you to unite them with your bitter
    sufferings, and thus perfect them by making
    them your own.
Amen.

Christian

A new day

Dear Lord, here is a new day you have given
me in which to love you and to help others
to love you.
Above all things help me to love and accept
your holy will.
Amen.

Christian

In difficult times

Teach me, O Lord, to do your will, for you
are my God.
Keep me, Lord, as the apple of your eye;
hide me in the shadow of your wings.
O Lord, blame us not for the iniquities of the
past; may your compassion quickly come
to us.
Amen.

Christian

Prayer for animals

God Our Heavenly Father,
You created the world to serve humanity's
    needs and to lead them to You.
By our own fault we have lost the beautiful
    relationship which we once had with all
    your creation.
Help us to see that by restoring our
    relationship with You we will also restore it
    with all Your creation.
Give us the grace to see all animals as gifts
    from You and to treat them with respect.
We pray for all animals who are suffering as a
    result of our neglect.
May the order You originally established be
    once again restored to the whole world
    through the intercession of the Glorious
    Virgin Mary, the prayers of St Francis and
    the merits of Your Son, Our Lord Jesus
    Christ who lives and reigns with You now
    and forever.
Amen.

St Francis of Assisi, c. 1181–1226

Christian

When someone is dying

My Lord God,
Even now resignedly and willingly, let us
 accept at Thy hand all anxieties, pains, and
 sufferings, for the death it brings.

Christian

Prayer for protection against
animal pests

O Lord,
By Thy power may these injurious animals be
 driven off and do no harm to any one.
May we be freed from the plague of these
 rodents (or worms, snails, plant lice, etc.) by
 Thy strong hand and may we joyously give
 thanks to Thy majesty.
Amen.

Christian

When trying to avoid sin

Dear Lord,
Have pity on us as we acknowledge our sins.
Lead us back to the way of holiness.
Protect us now and always from the wounds
   of sin.
May we ever keep safe in all its fullness the gift
   your love once gave us and your mercy now
   restores.
Amen.

Christian

Prayer when ill

O God, who are the only source of health and
   healing, the spirit of calm and the central
   peace of this universe.
Grant to me such a consciousness of your
   surrounding presence to give me health and
   strength and peace, through Jesus Christ
   our Lord.
Amen.

Christian

Prayer for God's mercy
in hard times

O Lord, show your mercy to me and gladden
    my heart.
I am like the man on the way to Jericho who
    was overtaken by robbers, wounded and left
    for dead.
O Good Samaritan, come to my aid, I am like
    the sheep that went astray.
O Good Shepherd, seek me out and bring me
    home in accord with your will.
Let me dwell in your house all the days of my
    life and praise you forever and ever.

St Jerome, c. 340–420

Buddhist

A blessing for ourselves

May I be filled with loving kindness.
May I be well.
May I be peaceful and at ease.
May I be happy.

Ancient Tibetan Buddhist meditation

Christian

Prayer to hear God's teaching

Please God, teach us, your humble servants, to
    do Your will in all our endeavors,
humbly in Your ever-lasting grace.
You are my light and delight, my Lord.
I am a sinner, and humbly beseech that we
    may put Your will into action.
Amen.

Christian

Prayer for those being held prisoner

Most gracious Father,
Bless with your special care all penitentiaries
    and homes of refuge.
Look with pity on those who are housed there.
Guide and protect those who have returned to
    the world.
Grant all of them true contrition for past sins,
    and strengthen them in their good
    resolutions.
Lead them along from grace to grace so that
    through the Holy Spirit they may persevere
    in the ways of obedience and humility, and
    in the struggle against evil thoughts and
    desires.
Amen.

St Cyprian of Carthage, c. 220–254

Christian

Prayer for a deceased relative or friend

I commend you almighty God, and entrust
  you to your Creator.
May you rest in the arms of the Lord who
  formed you from the dust of the Earth.
May Christ, the true Shepherd, embrace you
  as one of his flock.
May he forgive all your sins, and set you
  among those he has chosen.
And may you enjoy the vision of God forever.

Christian

Prayer for harmony with all living things

O God, grant us a deeper sense of fellowship
   with all living things and our brothers and
   sisters to whom you have given this earth as
   home.
May we realize that all these creatures also live
   for themselves and for you.
They too love the goodness of life, as we do,
   and serve you better in their way than we
   do in ours.
Amen.

St Basil of Caesarea, 329–379

Christian

Prayer in defence of life

Almighty God, Our Father, you have given us
life.
Grant us your blessings.
Give us the strength to defend human life
against every influence or action that may
threaten or weaken it.
Give us courage to proclaim the dignity of all
human life and to demand that society itself
give it protection.
We ask this in your name.
Amen.

Christian

A prayer for the driver

Dear God our Father,
Be with us now as we travel.
Be our safety every mile of the way.
Make us attentive, cautious and concerned
    about fellow travellers.
Make our highways safe and keep us from all
    danger.
Guide us to our destination today.
Amen.

Christian

Prayer for protection of the family

Jesus grant Your special graces to our family.
May our home be the shrine of peace, purity,
  love, labour and faith.
Protect and bless all of us, absent and present,
  living and dead.
Mary, pray to Jesus for our family and all the
  families of the world, to guard the cradle of
  the new born and the schools of the young.
Blessed Saint Joseph assist us by your prayers
  in all the necessities of life.
Amen.

Christian

Prayer when looking for employment

Dear God,
Please give me your help as I look for
   employment in this world.
Let me use the gifts and talents you have given
   me in giving service to others.
Do not abandon me, dear Father, in my
   search.
Grant me this favour so that I may return to
   you with praise and thanksgiving for your
   gracious assistance.
Amen.

Christian

Prayer for the family

St Joseph – God chose you as head of His
   holiest family.
Watch over us and extend your protection to
   our home.
May we remain united in the ties of Christian
   love and share the peace promised by Jesus
   to his disciples.
Grant that we may work together and love one
   another.
Amen.

Christian

Prayer for a good and just life

O Lord Jesus, gentle and humble of heart,
   full of compassion and maker of peace.
May we receive the word of the Gospel
   joyfully and live by your example as heirs to
   your kingdom.
Amen.

Christian

Prayer for generosity

Teach us to be generous, good Lord;
Teach us to serve You as You deserve.
To give and not to count the cost,
To fight and not to heed the wounds,
To toil and not to seek for rest,
To labor and not to ask for any reward save
    that of knowing we do Your will.

St Ignatius of Loyola, 1491–1556

Christian

Prayer for God's support

May He support us all the day long, till the
    shadows lengthen and the evening comes.
Till the busy world is hushed, the fever of life
    is over and our work is done.
Then in His mercy, may He give us a safe
    lodging, a holy rest and peace at least.

John Henry Newman, 1801–1890

Christian

Prayer for fathers

Saint Joseph, kindly protect those who
trustingly come to you.
You know their aspirations, their hardships,
their hopes.
They look to you because they know you will
understand and protect them.
You too knew trial, labor and weariness.
Assure those you protect that they do not
labor alone.
Teach them to find Jesus near them and to
watch over Him faithfully as you have
done.
Amen.

Pope John XXIII

Christian

Prayer on waking for God's protection and Christ's presence

As I arise today, may the strength of God pilot
    me, the power of God uphold me, and the
    wisdom of God guide me.
May the eye of God look before me, the ear of
    God hear me, and the word of God speak
    for me.
May the hand of God protect me, the way of
    God lie before me, the shield of God
    defend me, and the host of God save me.
Amen.

St Patrick of Ireland, 387–461

Christian

Prayer for harmony

God the Father, source of everything divine.
In you is tranquillity, peace and harmony.
Heal our divisions and restore us to the unity
   of love.
Let the bond of love and the ties of divine
   affection make us one in the Spirit.
We ask this through the grace, mercy, and
   compassion of your only Son, our Lord
   Jesus Christ.

St Dionysius of Alexandria, 190–268

Christian

Prayer for harvest and thanksgiving

O God, source and giver of all things,
You manifest Your infinite majesty, power and
    goodness in the earth about us; we give You
    honour and glory.
For the sun and the rain, for the manifold
    fruits of our fields, for the increase of our
    herds and flocks we thank You.
For the enrichment of our souls with divine
    grace, we are grateful.
We make this prayer through Christ our Lord.
Amen.

Christian

Prayer for help against spiritual enemies

O Lord I earnestly entreat you to assist me in
   the painful and dangerous conflict I sustain
   against my formidable foe.
Be with me, Lord, so that I may courageously
   fight and vanquish that proud spirit.
And having triumphed over the enemy of my
   salvation may I reside with you and the
   holy angels.
I praise the clemency of God who having
   refused mercy to the rebellious angels after
   their fall has granted repentance and
   forgiveness to fallen man.
Amen.

Christian

Prayer asking for help

O God, send forth your Holy Spirit into my
   heart that I may perceive, into my mind
   that I may remember, and into my soul
   that I may meditate.
Inspire me to speak with piety, holiness,
   tenderness and mercy.
Teach, guide and direct my thoughts and
   senses from beginning to end.
May your grace ever help and correct me, and
   may I be strengthened now with wisdom
   from on high, for the sake of your infinite
   mercy.
Amen.

St Anthony of Padua, 1195–1231

Christian

Prayer for life

Loving Father, Creator of life,
Help us to see anew the miracle and sacredness
   of all life and help us to protect this life
   with all Your goodness.
Amen.

Christian

Prayer for a safe pregnancy

Heavenly Father, who creates us in His own
 image.
We pray that not even the least among us
 should perish.
We beseech you to protect our little ones
 whom You have graciously granted unto us
 and bring to bear this grateful gift of life.
Amen.

Christian

Prayer for justice for all human beings

Almighty and eternal God,
May Your grace kindle in all of us a love for
   the many unfortunate people whom
   poverty and misery reduce to a condition of
   life unworthy of human beings.
Arouse in the hearts of those who call You
   Father a hunger and thirst for social justice.
Grant, O Lord, peace in our days: peace to
   souls, peace in families, peace to our
   country, and peace among nations.
Amen.

Pope Pius XII

Christian

Prayer for good conduct

O Lord Jesus,
Give me grace to make every effort to
    supplement faith with moral courage,
Knowledge with self-control,
Self-control with patience,
Patience with piety,
Piety with brotherly affection,
And brotherly affection with love.
May these virtues keep me both active and
    fruitful and bring me to knowledge of you,
    Lord Jesus Christ.
Amen.

Christian

Prayer for human dignity

O God, our Creator,
All life is in your hands from conception until
    death.
Help us to cherish our children, our share in
    creation.
May all people live and die in dignity and
    love.
Enlighten and be merciful toward those who
    fail to love, and give them peace.
Let freedom be tempered by responsibility,
    integrity and morality.

African (Yoruban)

Thanksgiving

Oh Divine One,
I give thanks to You,
The one who is as near as my heartbeat,
And more anticipated than my next breath.
Let Your wisdom become one with this vessel
   as I lift my voice in thanks for Your love.

Christian

Prayer for migrants and refugees

Father of the poor,
Help us in your work,
To take the side of the lowly,
To defend the newcomer,
To welcome the stranger.
Help us now to befriend the friendless,
Protect the weak children, and work for the
   rights of all.
Lord, on our journey home, bring us all
   together in peace, in justice, and in love,
   through Christ our Lord.
Amen.

Christian

Prayer for light in dark times

O Holy Spirit of God, take me as Thy
disciple; guide me, illuminate me,
sanctify me.
Bind my hands, that they may do no evil;
cover my eyes, that they may see it no
more; sanctify my heart, that evil may not
dwell within me.
Be Thou my God; be Thou my guide.
Wherever Thou lead me I will go; whatever
Thou forbids me I will renounce; and
whatever Thou commands me, in Thy
strength I will do.
Lead me, then, unto the fullness of Thy truth.
Amen.

Christian

Prayer for motherhood

Dear Lord,
Our marriage has not as yet been blessed with
a child, yet how much my husband and I
desire this gift.
Please hear our fervent pleas to the Creator of
life from whom all parenthood proceeds
and beseech Him to bless us with a child
whom we may raise as His child and heir
of heaven.
Amen.

Christian

Prayer for openness

Lord Jesus, open our ears and hearts today to
your message so that through the power of
your death and resurrection we may walk in
newness of life in accord with Your
teachings.
Amen.

Christian

Prayer for pardon

O Lord, the hour of your favor draws near,
   the day of your mercy and our salvation.
We acknowledge our sins and our offences
   always before us.
Blot out all our wrong doings and give us a
   new and steadfast spirit.
Restore us to your friendship and number us
   among the living who share the joy of you.
Amen.

Christian

Prayer for peace

O God, grant us that peace which the world
   cannot give, so that we may be obedient to
   your commands and under your protection
   enjoy peace in our days and freedom from
   fear of our enemies.
Amen.

Christian

When a friend or family member dies

May the souls of the faithful departed,
    through the mercy of God, rest in peace.
Amen.

Christian

For justice

O Lord Jesus Christ,
Grant us a measure of your Spirit.
Help us to
Obey your teaching,
Soothe anger,
Cultivate pity,
Overcome desire,
Increase love,
Cast off sorrow,
Shun vainglory,
Renounce revenge,
And not be afraid of death.
Let us ever entrust our spirit to the everlasting
    God who with you and the Holy Spirit
    lives and rules forever and ever.
Amen.

St Apollonius of Rome, d. 185

Christian

For the protection of family

O Lord, protect my family from all evil as you
    did the Holy Family.
Keep us ever united in the love of Christ,
    ever fervent in imitation of the virtue of our
    Blessed Lady, and always faithful in
    devotion to you.
Amen.

Christian

Prayer to redeem lost time

O my God! Source of all mercy!
While recalling the wasted years that are past,
I believe that You, Lord, can in an instant turn
    this loss to gain.
Please restore to me the time lost, giving me
    Your grace, both now and in the future,
    that I may appear before You in "wedding
    garments".
Amen.

St Teresa of Avila, 1515–82

Christian

Prayer for renewal

Lord, we are Your people, the sheep of Your
    flock.
Heal the sheep who are wounded,
Touch the sheep who are in pain,
Clean the sheep who are soiled,
Warm the lambs who are cold,
Calm the sheep who fear.
Renew us that we may help renew the face of
    the Earth.
Amen.

Christian

Prayer for reparation

Eternal Father, I ask you to expiate all the sins
    I have committed this day, and during all
    my life.
Please purify the good I have done in my poor
    way this day, and during all my life.
And make up for the good I ought to have
    done and that I have neglected this day and
    during all my life.
Amen.

Christian

To take life more slowly

Slow my pace, Lord.
Slow my life.
I am exhausted.
Give rest to my heart; bring calm to my
    feelings.
Set aside the problems of mind; soothe the
    aches of the heart; give rest to the body.

Christian

Prayer for souls in purgatory

Eternal Father,
I pray today in union with Masses said
    throughout the world that you have pity for
    all the holy souls in purgatory.
May the souls departed, through the mercy of
    God, rest in peace.
Amen.

Christian

Prayer for a death

O gentlest heart of Jesus, have mercy on the
    soul of thy departed servant.
Be not severe in Thy judgement, but let some
    drops of the Precious Blood fall upon the
    devouring flames, and send Your angels to
    conduct Your departed servant to a place of
    refreshment, light and peace.
Amen.

Christian

Prayer for the dead

Eternal rest grant unto them, O Lord,
    and let perpetual light shine upon them.
May the souls of the faithful departed,
    through the Mercy of God, rest in peace.
Amen.

Christian

Prayer for the spirit of work

O Lord! Obtain for me the grace to work in a
   spirit of penance to atone for my many sins;
To work conscientiously, putting the call of
   duty above my own inclinations.
To work with gratitude and joy, considering it
   an honor to use and develop by my labor
   the gifts I have received from God;
To work with order, peace, moderation and
   patience, without ever recoiling before
   weariness or difficulties.
Amen.

Christian

Prayer for strength in times of weakness

Lord Jesus Christ,
Cleanse from me my secret faults.
You know I am weak, both in soul and in body.
Give me strength, O Lord, in my frailty and
    sustain me in my sufferings.
Let me always be mindful of your blessings.

St Ephrem of Syria, 306–373

Christian

Prayer for travellers

O almighty and merciful God, who has
    commissioned Thine angels to guide and
    protect us.
Command them to be our assiduous
    companions from our setting out until our
    return.
To clothe us with their invisible protection; to
    keep from us all danger of collision, of fire,
    of explosion, of falls and bruises, and
    finally, having preserved us from all evil to
    guide us to our heavenly home.

Christian

A blessing for all

Give perfection to beginners,
Understanding to the little ones,
And help to those who are running their
    course.
Give sorrow to the negligent,
Fervor to the lukewarm,
And a good consummation to the perfect.

Christian

Blessing of bread

Lord Jesus Christ,
Graciously deign to bless this bread as Thou
    did bless the five loaves in the desert: that
    all who partake of it may have health of
    body and soul.
Who lives and reigns forever.
Amen.

Christian

When someone is unwell

Dear God,
We place our worries in your hands.
We place our sick under your care and
    humbly ask that you restore your servant to
    health again.
Amen.

Christian

Blessing of a house

Bless O Almighty God this house.
May health and purity, goodness and
    meekness, and every virtue reign here.
May all those who dwell here be filled with
    faithfulness to Thy law and with
    thanksgiving to God.
And may this blessing remain on this house
    and all who dwell here.

Christian

Blessing of a vehicle

Dear God, bless this vehicle with Thy right
    hand.
Send Thy holy angels to accompany it and
    may they keep from all evils those who ride
    in it.
Through Christ our Lord.
Amen.

Christian

Blessing of a sick animal

We call upon Thy mercy, O Lord;
Grant that this animal afflicted with disease,
    be restored to health in Thy name and by
    the power of Thy blessing.
May it languish in sickness no more and be
    Thou, O Lord, the protector of its life and
    the healer of its ailments.
Amen.

Christian

Blessing of food

Bless, O Lord this food.
Grant that all who partake of it may obtain
    health of body and safety of soul, through
    Christ our Lord.
Amen.

Christian

Prayer of thanks for people

God of Love, I thank you for the people in my
    life who are easy to love.
I thank you for my family and friends, who
    understand my actions, who support me in
    my decisions, and whose presence can lift
    the burden of a thorny day.

Help me with those who are difficult to love.
When they come at me with criticism and wild
    expectations, when they ignore me or try to
    bend me to their will, let me recognize their
    flaws and their dangers.
But then let me remember your attitude
    toward them, and lead me to see them in
    the light of your love.
Amen.

West African

For God's help

Help me in my faith, O Lord.
Help me not to seek too much fame, nor seek
   obscurity.
Help me to be proud.
To excel when I must.

Christian

Serenity prayer

God, grant me the serenity to accept the
   things I cannot change, the courage to
   change the things I can, and the wisdom to
   know the difference.
Living one day at a time, enjoying one
   moment at a time, accepting hardships as
   the pathway to peace, taking this sinful
   world as it is, not as I would have it.
Trusting that He will make all things right.
Amen.

Christian

Prayer to one's guardian angel

Dear Angel,
In his goodness God gave you to me to guide,
   protect and enlighten me, and to being me
   back to the right way when I go astray.
Encourage me when I am disheartened, and
   instruct me when I err.
Help me to become a better person, and some
   day be accepted into the company of angels
   and saints in heaven.
Amen.

Christian

A child's good morning prayer

Good morning God.
You usher in another day untouched, fresh
     and new.
Please help me so that this new day will renew
     me too.
But Lord, I am well aware, I can't make it on
     my own.
So take my hand and hold it tight, for I
     cannot walk alone.
Amen.

Christian

Prayer to an angel

Angel of God,
My Guardian dear,
To whom His love
Commits me here,
Ever this day
Be at my side,
To light and guard,
To rule and guide.

Christian

Prayer for a safe journey

Dear Lord, bless this journey which I
   undertake, that it may profit the health of
   my soul and body; that I may reach its end,
   and that, returning safe and sound, I may
   find my family in good health.
Amen.

Christian

Prayer to Saint Anthony of Padua
for finding a lost object

Saint Anthony, the patron of the poor and the
   helper of all who seek lost articles.
Help me to find the object I have lost.
Grant your gracious aid to all people who seek
   what they have lost and especially help
   those who seek to regain God's grace.
Amen.

Christian

Prayer to Saint Christopher for safe driving

I pray to Saint Christopher; protect all drivers
who transport those who bear Christ within
them.
Amen.

Christian

Prayer for protection against miscarriage

Dear Lord in Heaven,
You know the dangers that await unborn
infants.
Intercede for me that I may avoid miscarriage
and bring forth a healthy baby who will
become a true child of God.
May You also pray for all mothers, that they
may bring a healthy new life into the world.
Amen.

Christian

Prayer for a healthy pregnancy

Dear Saint Gerard, who has been raised up by
    God as the patron and protector of
    expectant mothers.
Preserve me in the dangers of motherhood,
    and shield the child I now bear, that it may
    be brought safely to the light of day and
    receive the sacrament of baptism.

Christian

Prayer for mothers

Dear God,
Intercede for all mothers in our day so that
    they may learn to draw their children to
    God.
Teach them how to remain close to their
    children, and how to reach those sons and
    daughters who have sadly gone astray.
Amen.

Christian

Prayer for the world's beauty

Praised be my Lord and God, with all His
   creatures, and especially our brother the
   sun, who brings us the day and brings us
   the light.
Fair is he, and he shines with great splendor.
O Lord, he is a sign to us of you!
Praised be my Lord for our sister the moon,
   and for this stars, set clear and lovely in the
   heaven.

St Francis of Assisi, c. 1181–1226

Christian

We adore Thee

We adore Thee,
Most holy Lord Jesus Christ,
Here and in all Thy churches that are in the
   whole world,
And we bless Thee;
Because by Thy holy cross Thou hast
   redeemed the world.
Amen.

St Francis of Assisi, c. 1181–1226

Christian

Prayer of Saint Francis of Assisi

Lord, make me an instrument of your peace.
Where there is hatred, let me sow love;
Where there is injury, pardon;
Where there is doubt, faith;
Where there is despair, hope;
Where there is darkness, light;
And where there is sadness, joy.

O Divine Master, grant that I may not so
    much seek to be consoled as to console;
To be understood as to understand;
To be loved as to love.
For it is in giving that we receive;
It is in pardoning that we are pardoned;
And it is in dying that we are born to eternal
    life.
Amen.

St Francis of Assisi, c. 1181–1226

Christian

Despair prayer

Lord, I am in this world to show Your mercy
to others.
I will glorify You by making known how good
You are to sinners, that Your mercy is
boundless and that no sinner no matter
how great his offences should have reason
to despair of pardon.
If I have grievously offended You, My
Redeemer, let me not offend You even
more by thinking that You are not kind
enough to pardon Me.
Amen.

St Claude de la Colombière, 1641–82

Christian

For Jesus to watch over us

Watch, O Lord, over those who sleep tonight.
Tend our sick ones and rest our weary ones.
May we wake safely in the morning to start a
new day and all for Your love's sake.
Amen.

Christian

Prayer at the end of the day

Jesus Christ my God, I adore you and I thank
   you for all the graces you have given me
   this day.
I offer you my sleep and all the moments of
   this night, and I implore you to keep me
   safe from sin.
To this end I place myself in your sacred side
   and under the mantle of our Lady, my
   Mother.
Let your holy angels surround me and keep
   me in peace; and let your blessing be upon
   me.
Amen.

St Alphonsus Maria de Liguori, 1696–1787

Islamic

Prayer for pardon

My God,
Let the cloud of Thy mercy cast its shadow
    upon my sins and send the billow of Thy
    clemency flowing over my faults!

Christian

A prayer for forgiveness at bedtime

O Lord our God,
If during this day I have sinned, whether in
    word or deed or thought,
Forgive me all, for thou art good and love
    mankind.
Grant me peaceful and undisturbed sleep, and
    raise me up again tomorrow.
For Thou art blessed.
Amen.

Buddhist

Prayer for good conduct

May I be a protector to those without
   protection,
A leader for those who journey,
And a boat, a bridge, a passage
For those desiring the further shore.
May the pain of every living creature
Be completely cleared away.
May I be the doctor and the medicine
And may I be the nurse
For all sick beings in the world
Until everyone is healed.

Shantideva Buddhist

Christian

Thanksgiving after deliverance
from trouble

Almighty and merciful God,
I most humbly and heartily thank thee that
   thou hast heard my humble prayer, and
   graciously vouchsafed to deliver me from
   my trouble and misery.
Amen.

Christian

Prayer of the married

My bountiful God, I beseech Thee, listen to
   my humble prayer,
that I may ever feel that the married state is
   holy and that I must keep it holy.
Grant Thy grace that I may never sin against
   the love of this marriage.
Foster between us the spirit of understanding
   and of peace, that no strife, quarrel or
   misunderstanding, may arise between us.
Amen.

Christian

Prayer before a journey

O Lord Jesus Christ our God,
Deliver and protect me from all danger,
   misfortune and temptation; that being so
   defended by Thy divine power, I may have
   a peaceful and successful journey and arrive
   safely at my destination.
For in thee I put my trust and hope, now and
   ever.
Amen.

Christian

For those who care for us

Our Father, Who art in heaven,
Bless my father and mother, my guardians,
    and those who are in authority over me, for
    their love and tender care for me, and the
    benefits I receive at their hands.
Help me to be respectful and obedient to
    them in all matters.
Give me grace to perform all my duties
    carefully and faithfully.
Amen.

Islamic

For guidance

My God,
Have mercy upon Thy lowly slave of silent
    tongue and few good works, obligate him
    through Thy plentiful graciousness, shelter
    him under Thy plenteous shade!
O Generous, O Beautiful,
O Most Merciful of the merciful!

Islamic

For deliverance for wrongdoing

My God,
Though the sins of Thy servant are ugly,
Thy pardon is beautiful.

Islamic

For the right path through life

My God,
Place me among the chosen, the good.
Join me to
The righteous,
The pious,
The first to reach generous gifts,
The swift to come upon good things,
The workers of the abiding acts of
    righteousness,
The strivers after elevated degrees!
Thou art powerful over everything and
    disposed to respond!
By Thy mercy,
O Most Merciful of the merciful!

Islamic

For protection

My God,
Empty us not of Thy defending,
Strip us not of Thy guarding,
And protect us from the roads of destruction,
For we are in Thy eye and under Thy wing!

Islamic

For affirmation of belief

He who gives to a servant and takes him to his
     wish when he expectantly hopes for what is
     within Him.
He brings him near and close when he
     approaches Him.
Covers over his sin and cloaks it when he
     shows it openly, and satisfies and suffices
     him when he has confidence in Him!

Buddhist

Respect for each other

Let no one despise another,
Let no one out of anger or resentment
    wish suffering on anyone at all.
Just as a mother with her own life
    protects her child from harm,
So within yourself, let grow
    a boundless love for all creatures.

Buddhist

On sharing and making others happy

Thousands of candles can be lighted from a
    single candle, and the life of the candle will
    not be shortened.
Happiness never decreases by being shared.

Islamic

For unity and faith

By the token of time through the ages,
Verily, man is in loss,
Except such as have faith, and do righteous
    deeds,
And join together in the mutual teaching of
    truth,
And of patience and constancy.

Islamic

Refuge from all things bad

I seek refuge with the Lord of the Dawn,
From the mischief of created things;
And from the mischief of darkness as it
    overspreads; and from the mischief of the
    envious one as he practises envy.

Islamic

For protection

I seek refuge with the Lord and Cherisher of
    Mankind,
The King of Mankind,
The Lord of Mankind,
From the mischief of the whisperer of Evil,
    who withdraws after his whisper,
The same who whispers into the hearts of
    Mankind.

Hindu

Morning blessing

O! Mother Earth, who has the ocean as clothes
    and mountains and forests on her body,
    who is the wife of Lord Vishnu, I bow to
    you.
Please forgive me for touching you with my
    feet.

Traditional

Taoist

On small beginnings

To put the world in order,
    we must first put the nation in order;

To put the nation in order,
    we must first put the family in order;

To put the family in order,
    we must first cultivate our personal life;

We must first set our hearts right.

Confucius, 551–479 BC

Hindu

Oh Almighty

You alone are our mother and father.
You alone are our friend and close companion.
You alone are our knowledge, wealth and all
   in all.

Prapannagita 28

Hindu

On God's omnipresence

This ritual is One.
The food is One.
We who offer the food are One.
The fire of hunger is also One.
All action is One.
We who understand this are One.

Traditional blessing

Hindu

In praise of life

Not Christian or Jew or Muslim
Not Hindu, Buddhist, Sufi, or Zen,
Not any religion or cultural system.
I am not from the east or the west,
Not out of the ocean or up from the ground,
Not natural or ethereal,
Not composed of elements at all.
I do not exist, am not an entity in this world
    or the next.
Did not descend from Adam and Eve or any
    origin story.
My place is the placeless, a trace of the
    traceless,
Neither body nor soul.
I belong to the beloved,
Have seen the two worlds as one
And that one call to and know,
First, last, outer, inner
Only that breath breathing human being.

Sufi mystic Jelaluddin Rumi, 13th century

Hindu

Oh Almighty, You are infinite

Oh Almighty, You are infinite, the universe is
  also infinite.
From infinite the infinite has come out!
Having taken infinite out of the infinite, the
  infinite remains.

Ishawashya Upanishad 1

Non-denominational

The great invocation

From the point of Light within the Mind of
    God
Let light stream forth into the minds of men.
Let Light descend on Earth.
From the point of Love within the Heart of
    God
Let love stream forth into the hearts of men.
Let the Plan of Love and Light work out.
And may it seal the door where evil dwells.
Let Light and Love and Power restore the Plan
    on Earth.

In Buddhist, Hindu, Muslim, and Jewish
translations of the Great Invocation, the name of
the Coming One is spoken as Lord Maitreya,
Krishna, the Imam Mahdi and the Messiah.

Hindu

For couples

United your resolve, united your hearts,
May your spirits be at one,
That you may long together dwell
In unity and concord.

Rig Veda: the final mantra

Hindu

Prayer for guidance

May he bestow prudence on all of us.
May he inspire us towards righteous cause.
May he guide us to speak the truth.
May he make us conscious about spirituality.

Grama Geeta

Divine Life Society

Universal prayer

O Adorable Lord of Mercy and Love!
Salutations and prostration unto Thee.
Thou art Omnipresent, Omnipotent and
    Omniscient.
Thou art Satchidananda (Existence-
    Consciousness-Bliss Absolute).
Thou art the Indweller of all beings.
Grant us an understanding heart, equal vision,
    balanced mind, faith, devotion and
    wisdom.
Grant us inner spiritual strength to resist
    temptations and to control the mind.
Free us from egoism, lust, greed, hatred, anger
    and jealousy.
Fill our hearts with divine virtues.

Sri Swami Sivananda, 1887–1963

Hindu

For continuing guidance

Oh Almighty, stay by my side.
Naughty or good, I am Thy child.

Paramahansa Yogananda

Hindu

Prayer of devotion

O my Lord, best of the givers of benediction,
If You at all want to bestow a desirable
   benediction upon me,
Then I pray from Your Lordship that within
   the core of my heart there be no material
   desires.
Sri Prahlada Maharaja

Hindu

Prayer for guidance

Oh Almighty, lead us from the unreal [falsity]
to the real [truth], from darkness to light
From mortality to immortality.
Oh Almighty may there be peace . . .
   peace . . . peace

Brihdaranyaka Upanisada 1: 3: 27

Hindu

For health, happiness and peace

Oh Almighty.
May everybody be happy.
May all be free from ailments.
May we see what is auspicious.
May no one be subject to miseries.

Rig Veda 4: 11: 51, 3700 BC

Hindu

For guidance

O God, the Giver of Life,
Remover of pains and sorrows,
Bestower of happiness, and
Creator of the Universe;
Thou art luminous, pure and adorable;
We meditate on Thee.
May Thou inspire and guide our intellect in
    the right direction.

*The Gayatri mantra to the Lord Sun
in the Cosmos*

Non-denominational

Universal prayer

And we call on the Great Nameless One:
Hear us, oh friend.
To whom, in our mortal sight,
We have given names to the Nameless.
Through the countless eons of time
We cry out through millions of throats,
And in our one voice we call to You:
And we ask You hear our call.

Matthew Yrigoyen, Japan

Hindu

Prayer for guidance

Oh Almighty,
We meditate upon the adorable radiant, the
    divine sun.
May he unfold and give direction to our
    intellects to go on the right path!

Rig Veda 3: 62: 10, 4,000 BC

Christian

For God's love

Take, O Lord, and receive my entire liberty,
my memory, my understanding and my
whole will.
All that I am and all that I possess You have
given me.
I surrender it all to You to be disposed of
according to Your will.
Give me only Your love and Your grace; with
these I will be rich enough, and will desire
nothing more.

St Ignatius of Loyola, 1491–1556

Christian

Prayer before commencing any task

Almighty God, I pray thee to direct me to
accomplish this task, and whatever I may
undertake to do, faithfully and diligently,
according to thy will, so that it may be
profitable to myself and others, and to the
glory of thy Holy Name.
Amen.

Christian

For faith

I would be true, for there are those who trust
  me.
I would be pure, for there are those who care.
I would be strong, for there is much to suffer.
I would be brave, for there is much to dare.
I would be brave, for there is much to dare.

I would be friend of all – the foe, the
  friendless;
I would be giving, and forget the gift;
I would be humble, for I know my weakness;
I would look up, and laugh, and love and lift.
I would look up, and laugh, and love and lift.

I would be faithful through each passing
  moment;
I would be constantly in touch with God;
I would be strong to follow where He leads
  me;
I would have faith to keep the path Christ
  trod;
I would have faith to keep the path Christ
  trod.

Howard Arnold Walter, Japan, 1906

Christian

For teaching faith

My Lord, I know not what I ought to ask of
    Thee.
Thou and Thou alone knows my needs.
Thou loves me more than I am able to love
    Thee.
O Father, grant unto me, Thy servant, all
    which I cannot ask.
My heart is open to Thee.
Thou sees my needs of which I myself am
    unaware.
Behold and lift me up!
In Thy presence I stand, awed and silenced by
    Thy will and Thy judgments.
No other desire is mine but to fulfil Thy will.
Teach me how to pray.
Amen.

Prayer of Philaret,
Metropolitan of Moscow, 1782–1867

Christian

For Africa

God Bless Africa;
Guard her children;
Guide her leaders
And give her peace, for Jesus Christ's sake.
Amen.

Christian

For those at sea

Almighty, Everlasting God,
The Protector of all those who put their trust
in Thee:
Hear our prayers on behalf of Thy servants
who sail their vessels upon the seas.
Grant them courage, and a devotion to fulfil
their duties, that they may better serve Thee
and their native land.
Grant them a good ship's spirit.
Bless all their kindred and loved ones from
whom they are separated.
Amen.

Anon

African (Pygmy)

God's infinity

In the beginning was God,
Today is God,
Tomorrow will be God.
Who can make an image of God?
He has no body.
He is the word which comes out of your
    mouth.
That word
It is no more,
It is past, and still it lives.
So is God.

Christian

Prayer to your guardian angel

Guardian Angel from heaven so bright,
Watching beside me to lead me to right,
Fold your wings around me,
And guard me with love,
Softly sing your songs to me
Of heaven above.
Amen.

Buddhist

A blessing

May you be filled with loving kindness.
May you be well.
May you be peaceful and at ease.
May you be happy.

Ancient Tibetan Buddhist blessing

African (Yoruban)

Thanksgiving

To our Gods of old, we bless the ground that
    you trod in search of our freedom.
We bless your presence in our lives and in our
    hearts.
Take of this offering to your delight, and be
    filled with our prayers of thanksgiving.
May our lives remain as full as our hearts on
    this day.

Christian

The Lord's Prayer

Our father which art in Heaven,
Hallowed be thy name,
Thy kingdom come,
Thy will be done,
In Earth as it is in Heaven,
Give us this day our daily bread,
And forgive us our trespasses,
As we forgive those who trespass against us;
And lead us not into temptation;
But deliver us from evil:
For thine is the kingdom,
The power and the glory
For ever and ever.
Amen.

Book of Common Prayer, 1662

Christian

Praise for Jesus

There is a balm in Gilead
To make the wounded whole;
There is a balm in Gilead
To heal the sin-sick soul.

Some times I feel discouraged,
And think my work's in vain,
But then the Holy Spirit
Revives my soul again.

If you can't preach like Peter,
If you can't pray like Paul,
Just tell the love of Jesus,
And say He died for all.

African-American spiritual

Christian

Prayer for migrants

O Lord, defend the human rights and dignity
  of people on the move.
Help us to advocate social remedies to their
  problems, and to foster opportunities for
  their spiritual and religious growth.
We pledge ourselves to resist injustices against
  newcomers, to assist them in their need,
  and to welcome them into our nation and
  our community of faith as fellow pilgrims
  on the journey to the Father.
Amen.

Daoist

For peace

If there is to be peace in the world,
    there must be peace in the nations.
If there is to be peace in the nations,
    there must be peace in the cities.
If there is to be peace in the cities,
    there must be peace between neighbors.
If there is to be peace between neighbors,
    there must be peace in the home.
If there is to be peace in the home,
    there must be peace in the heart.

Lao Tse, 6th century BC

Christian

To be a better listener

Dear God,
We do not listen enough to each other.
Teach me to listen as Your Son listened to
    everyone who spoke with Him.
Remind me that You are trying to reach me
    through my partner in conversation.
Your truth, Your love, Your goodness are
    seeking me in the truth, love and goodness
    being communicated.
Teach me to be still, Lord, that I may truly hear
    my brothers and sisters – and, in them, You.
Amen.

Hindu

For protection and peace

Oh Almighty,
May he protect all of us.
May he cause us to enjoy.
May we acquire strength together.
May our knowledge become brilliant.
May we not hate each other!

Kathopanisada 2: 6: 19, 1,400 BC

Christian

Prayer for workers

Dear God, thank you for the clothes I wear
    today.
Please send the joy of your love into the lives
    of those who made them and all the other
    good things in my life.
May those who control industry be just and
    fair to their workers.
Help us to love one another as you love us.
In the name of Jesus Christ our Lord.
Amen.

Buddhist

For accepting God's will

Pray to put an end to hope and fear:
If it's better for me to be ill,
I pray for the blessing of illness.
If it's better for me to recover,
I pray for the blessing of recovery.
If it's better for me to die,
I pray for the blessing of death.

Jamgon Kongtrul Rinpoche